Spiritual Truths for
Overcoming
Adversity

Spiritual Truths for
Overcoming Adversity

By Greg Hinnant

BRIDGE • LOGOS *Publishers*
South Plainfield, NJ

Spiritual Truths for Overcoming Adversity
by Greg Hinnant
ISBN 0-88270-690-X
Library of Congress Catalog Card Number 95-78188
Copyright © 1995 by BRIDGE • LOGOS Publishers

Published by:
BRIDGE • LOGOS Publishers
2500 Hamilton Blvd.
South Plainfield, NJ 07080

Contents

Dedication...vii
Foreword..ix
Preface..xiii

1. Acceptance..1
2. The Power to Endure...................................9
3. Made Strong Through Adversity...................15
4. Teaching and Testing................................25
5. Another Chance.......................................37
6. God Is Watching.......................................43
7. Rise Above It!..51
8. Take the Serpent by the Tail!.....................63
9. Determination... 73
10. God's Sanding Process.............................83
11. At Your Right Hand.................................89
12. Merciless Criticism..................................99
13. Refreshing Spirituality............................105
14. When Relief is on the Way.......................115
15. "Sans Blessings" Saints............................123
16. Where to Turn When Others Turn Away...131
17. Trouble in the Center of His Will...............139
18. Victory the Hard Way..............................147
19. The Price of Fruitfulness..........................155
20. We Must Be Courageous..........................161
21. God Empowers Those Who Take a Stand!.173
22. When the Clash Comes.............................183
23. A Matrimonial Message............................189
24. He Wounds and Heals..............................195
25. Thinning The Ranks.................................203
26. Shall He Find This Belief?.........................211

God forges us on an anvil of adversity for a purpose known only to Him. That is the way He prepares us for life.

J. E. Broyhill

Foreword

A few years ago, I experienced some very difficult circumstances. While on the board of the church I was then attending, I felt challenged by the Lord to take a stand for His high standards and to fear Him only, not men. I obeyed, but paid a high price for my obedience. This left me wondering why the Lord permitted all the negative reactions I received, particularly since I did what I believed He called me to do.

During this time, I clung to the Lord, received comfort from the Psalms, and regularly read messages by Greg Hinnant that were published in the *Herald of His Coming*. Those messages were a great blessing to me. By presenting practical principles from the Word of God, they helped me first *survive* and then *overcome* my difficulties. The messages reaffirmed to me that the Lord is close to those who are humble and of a contrite heart. They stressed the necessity to forgive and to praise the Lord for who He is, even when we are besieged by great problems. They encouraged me to persevere and to trust the Lord at all times. They challenged me to set my affections on things above, not on things on the earth. They helped me to more clearly see the Lord, who Himself overcame, and with whose help, I realized, I could also overcome.

After this experience, God showed Himself exceedingly faithful in ways that I could not have imagined during my pain and suffering. I was struck particularly by His ability to make "all things work together for good" (Romans 8:28), even the most negative experiences and things that men meant for evil against me. He turned my difficulties into character growth and, later, ministry opportunities. Based on my church-related trial, the Lord gave me several church-related messages and, to my surprise, opened doors for their publication in well-known Christian magazines in the United States and Great Britain. God is so good! To them that "mourn in Zion" He can give "beauty for ashes, the oil of joy for mourning, the garment of praise for a spirit of heaviness . . . that he might be glorified" (Isaiah 61:3).

These blessings prompted me to contact Greg Hinnant and suggest that he seek to have some of his writings published in book form so that they might help a wider audience of Christians. Thus began the process that led to the publication of this book.

Greg Hinnant is a lay minister, a Christian writer who pastors a home church in High Point, North Carolina. He diligently seeks the Lord in his endeavors to glean precious principles from the Word of God and pass them on to believers through the printed page. I appreciate the gift God has given him to present biblical truth clearly, simply, and in a practical, useful way.

The principles contained in *Spiritual Truths for Overcoming Adversity* can make the difference between success and failure in our trials, no matter what kind or how difficult they are. Often, of course, they require denying oneself and taking up the cross, along with persistence, until a breakthrough comes.

May this book help many to pass through the storms of life victoriously by faithfully applying God's Word and by trusting in the grace and power of Jesus Christ.

Ernst Lutz, Ph.D.
Rockville, Maryland
February 1995

(Ernst Lutz, a Swiss citizen, is a Senior Economist with the World Bank in Washington, D.C. He has written Christian pieces and book reviews for *Charisma, Ministries Today, Renewal,* and the *Morning Star Journal.*)

Preface

Though we would prefer to live in continuous prosperity, adversity cannot be avoided in the way of true Christianity. In a fallen world, loyalty to God and His Word carries with it a permanently fixed price tag. Jesus taught, "Tribulation or persecution ariseth because of the Word" (Matthew 13:21). When the enemy comes in like a flood, our reaction is crucial. It makes or breaks us as disciples of Jesus Christ.

Satan attacks serious Christians with a set purpose in view. He seeks to cause us to become offended with God, to end our fellowship with Him, to halt the development of our Christian character, and to prevent us from bearing further fruit unto God. If we fail to overcome our trials, Satan's objectives are realized.

God permits Satan's onslaughts for His own equally clear purpose. He is using the enemy and his agents to train us in scriptural thinking and spiritual living, and to establish us as full-fledged overcomers. When our season of testing arrives, if we sit down with Jacob and sob, "All these things are against me" (Genesis 42:36), we will never overcome. But if we learn the fundamental secret of accepting every circumstance as being from the hand of God, and determine to keep His word patiently, we will rise above the wiles of the enemy every time. With each new spiritual victory we will grow in knowledge of God, strength of character, discernment, spiritual authority, and Christian compassion. In this way, God prepares us to rule eternally with Christ.

But to overcome, and thus qualify to rule with Christ, we must have *spiritual understanding* concerning our various trials—we must look at them from God's viewpoint. Nothing else will hold us steady in the time of trouble: "Understanding shall keep thee" (Proverbs 2:11). The Bible is the only source of this precious spiritual understanding and we must constantly turn to it for help in difficult times.

Each chapter in this book contains spiritual truths mined from the pages of the Bible. These simple-yet-powerful eternal truths are capable of sustaining us when the winds, rains, and floods beat vehemently against our house of faith. For frightened Christian pilgrims caught in such storms of adversity, these truths illuminate God's pathway through the darkness and show us what the Lord would have us think, say, and do. If faithfully and tenaciously obeyed, they will bring us safely through to the end of every test.

Originally written as individual messages, each chapter has been rewritten for inclusion in this book. Born in the study of the Scriptures, proven by the fires of testing, and confirmed by having blessed many, these spiritual truths are offered here to those who earnestly seek to overcome the adversities set before them.

Greg Hinnant
High Point, North Carolina
August 1995

1

Acceptance

*In every thing give thanks: for this is the will
of God in Christ Jesus concerning you.*

(1 Thessalonians 5:18)

We either accept or reject everything we meet
with daily. As life acts upon us, we react. It's this
basic reaction that God is concerned with. In short,
the Bible tells us how to react to life.

Our natural reaction is to resist, for all of us are
resisters by nature: "Ye stiff-necked . . . ye do always
resist the Holy Spirit; as your fathers did, so do ye"
(Acts 7:51)—"Ye fight and war" (James 4:2). From
the womb we strive, argue, rebel, protest, and fight.
We need no training, no education in the art of
resistance. It comes naturally. The 'old man' in each
of us has an inborn aversion for all forms of trouble
or change. We go to all lengths to avoid trouble.
With the utmost cleverness, we dodge, duck, and
deny. And when undesirable change confronts us,
we reach for our sword to combat this intruder.

Through Redemption, God has undertaken the enormous task of transforming confirmed resisters into practicing acceptors. By commanding us to give thanks in everything, He seeks to instill in us the habit of accepting all things as from Him: "In every thing give thanks; for this is the will of God in Christ Jesus concerning you" (1 Thessalonians 5:18). Some examples of this are found in the Book of Job, where Job's reactions to his problems are recorded: "The Lord gave, and the Lord hath taken away" (Job 1:21)—"Shall we receive good at the hand of God, and shall we not receive evil?" (Job 2:10).

Giving thanks to God in all things is acknowledging and accepting His sovereignty and wisdom. It is the only way we can obtain God's wisdom to help us in time of need. To fail to give thanks is to fail to accept. And to fail to accept is to reject. When we reject trouble or undesired change, we cut ourselves off from God's help. *Only acceptance makes God's wisdom accessible.* That is, when we accept things as from Him, God immediately gives us His mind in the matter at hand.

For example, when Abraham accepted his severe test and took the knife to slay his son, Isaac, the angel of the Lord stopped his hand and opened his eyes to see the ram caught in the thicket (Genesis 22:13). God had a way of escape already prepared for Abraham, but he was not shown it until he fully accepted the painful obedience God called for. Similarly, when we fully accept our troublesome trials, suddenly we see the way of escape God has provided for us (1 Corinthians 10:13). *Acceptance opens our eyes.* When we acknowledge the Lord and

2

decide to obey, and put full trust in Him, He opens the eyes of our understanding. The instant we accept, we discern. Yielding brings immediate insight.

James 1:2-5 confirms this principle: "My brethren, count it all joy when ye fall into various trials . . . If any of you lack wisdom, let him ask of God, who giveth to all men liberally . . . and it shall be given him." If we joyfully accept our problems when we fall into various trials, then we may ask God for wisdom and He will give it to us. But if we refuse to look up and acknowledge God in the midst of the trouble at hand—the unexpected, the unwanted, the mean—we stay in the dark.

Resistance blinds us. It leaves us carnally minded, seeing only the outward, the natural, the human. We see only stubborn people and unsolved problems. Like Balaam, we're totally unaware of the angel of the Lord standing in the way (Numbers 22:31). We think only of our wants, not God's will; our comfort, not the needs of others; our immediate relief, not God's eternal purposes.

Acceptance isn't passivity. God doesn't want us to lie down and play dead, allowing everyone and everything to run over us. The fatalistic mentality that proclaims "what will be, will be," neither pleases God nor accomplishes His will. He seeks strong vessels, not limp dishrags. He doesn't approve of apathetic souls. He calls us to fight, not naturally, but spiritually; not in our ways and strength, but in His ways, His wisdom, His power; not to have our own way, but to insist that He has His way: "Thy will be done . . . in earth" (Luke 11:2). This is the good fight of faith. As the much-afflicted apostle Paul told his disciple, Timothy, "I have fought a good fight . . . I have kept the faith" (2 Timothy 4:7).

Paradoxically, to fight a good fight and keep the faith, we must not resist—or rebel against our circumstances. When we do, we don't fight in the proper way. When our basic reaction to trouble is to reject it outright, we neither think wisely nor act swiftly in the heat of trial. We become offended; fear and discouragement set in; and we lie down and quit. Then the devil and the workers of iniquity promptly trample us under their feet. But when we accept adversity as being allowed by God to train us, we see clearly how God would have us do spiritual battle. Consequently, we stand. We hear from heaven, make wise decisions, take bold action, confound our enemies, defeat the devil's plan, and overcome!

The man who rebels against his tests succumbs constantly to Satan's subtle strategy. The wiles of the devil are always intended to provoke us to disobey Christ's commands. Jesus said, "But I say unto you that ye resist not evil" (Matthew 5:39). In this context, evil means *adversity, injustice, affliction.* By resisting adversity, then, we are disobeying our Lord. That's exactly what the enemy wants. By our disobedience, we put ourselves over onto his ground. Having yielded to the spirit of disobedience, we become subject to the arch disobeyer: "Know ye not that to whom ye yield yourselves servants to obey, his servants ye are whom ye obey, whether of sin . . . or of obedience?" (Romans 6:16). If we accept and stand, we overcome. But when we rise up to fight, we come under. To fight in the natural is to lose in the spiritual. If we disobey Jesus, Satan wins.

After being grievously wronged and insulted by Nabal, David hastily gave the order, "Gird ye on every man his sword," and went forth to take vengeance (1 Samuel 25:13). When Abigail, Nabal's wife, met David, he was headed straight for spiritual failure. Had he not yielded to her wise counsel, he would have played right into the devil's hands, displeased God, and possibly lost His approval. Satan's strategy, operating through the man Nabal, would have been successful. And the enemy would have had a legitimate reproach to bring against the Lord.

Without doubt, acceptance is the great key to becoming a full-fledged overcomer. An overcomer is one who, above all else, is convinced that God controls every single thing that breaks through the hedge to touch his life: "Hast not thou made an hedge about him, and about his house, and about all that he hath on every side?" (Job 1:10). In the face of all adversity, the overcomer says, "Ye thought evil against me; but God meant it unto good" (Genesis 50:20). The overcomer accepts what others reject; where they rebel, he yields; where they harden their necks, he bends and submits to the yoke of Jesus; where they turn back, he presses on; where they fall offended, he stands "approved unto God" (2 Timothy 2:15).

The overcomer realizes that to reject his tests is to fail before he has even begun to be examined. Therefore, his first reaction in all situations is to accept what has happened as from the Lord. The fundamental revelation, "This thing is from me"

(1 Kings 12:24), is permanently imbedded in his mind. Therefore, he looks up and says, "Thank you, Lord." He then seeks God's mind in the matter and proceeds to act from the spiritual viewpoint, overcoming all things—his own old nature, his supernatural enemies, his natural opponents, and the devil himself.

> Judas then, having received a band of men and officers from the chief priests and Pharisees, cometh . . .
>
> (John 18:3)

> Then Simon Peter, having a sword, drew it, and smote the high priest's servant, and cut off his right ear. . . .
> Then said Jesus unto Peter, Put up thy sword into the sheath; the cup which my Father hath given me, shall I not drink it?
>
> (John 18:10-11)

In the garden, Peter resisted and Jesus accepted. Peter fell, while Jesus stood; he came under while Jesus came over. Peter was gripped with fear and panic, while Jesus remained calm in faith. Peter rebelled and therefore could not see the hand of God in it all. Jesus accepted the evil as from above and therefore endured as seeing Him who is invisible.

For the sorrow Peter was experiencing, he collapsed. For the joy set before Jesus, He stood and walked steadily forward. Because Peter resisted, he failed in the fiery trial. Because Jesus accepted, He overcame everything and everyone—Judas, Pilate, the chief priests, the bloodthirsty crowd, the Roman executioners, the mocking onlookers, the thief who reviled him, the devil, and death itself. What more could He have overcome?

After the Lord's resurrection, Peter experienced a second conversion. Not a religious conversion to faith in Christ—he had already experienced that—but an attitude conversion, a distinct change in his basic outlook on life. Peter was transformed from a typically human resister into an unusually spiritual acceptor who could then be used by the Lord to help others: "When thou art converted, strengthen thy brethren" (Luke 22:32). He put away his sword permanently. From that point on, Peter received every cup his heavenly Father gave him, even as Jesus did, and grew steadily in the grace of acceptance, being constantly "conformed to the image of his Son" (Romans 8:29).

Brothers and sisters, we must follow Peter's footsteps and enter into the conversion he experienced. When we fall into various trials, we must train ourselves to react from the spiritual viewpoint. We must deliberately *think*, "Count it all joy," instead of "I can't take any more." We must deliberately *say*, "Thank you, Lord," instead of, "Oh no, not this again!" We must deliberately submit to God's tests and resist the devil rather than *submit* to the devil by rebelling against our tests. Then we, as Peter, will be increasingly conformed to the image of God's Son.

Let us, henceforth, put away our sword of resistance, accept every cup our Father sends, and overcome.

2

The Power to Endure

Be assured that the testing of your faith leads to power of endurance.

(James 1:3, *Weymouth* translation)

The more tests we pass through in obedience, the more spiritual power we gain.

Various trials are God's special means of strengthening us in Christ. Oh yes, we gain edification from meditation in the Word, prayer, and the fellowship of the saints, but this can evaporate quickly if we don't learn to pass our tests in the daily circumstances God arranges for us. Permanent strength of character comes only by passing through many tests of faith and patience in a submitted, obedient frame of mind. George Mueller, who cared for 2,500 orphans a day by faith alone, said, "The *only* way to learn strong faith is to endure great trials. I have learned my faith by standing firm amid severe testings."

The power to endure is the ability to bear stress with ease, to be in distress without distress being in you. It's God's supernatural grace manifested in us. Situations that wear out others don't bother us. We go through the fire, but are not burned, neither is the smell of smoke detected upon us (Daniel 3:1-30; 6:22-23). We walk calmly and steadily through the midst of the most dreaded difficulties conceivable without mental, physical, or emotional damage. In fearful circumstances, we're calm and unafraid; in offensive situations, we're not offended; when faced with a deadline, we're not at our wits' end; when repeatedly wronged, we're miraculously free from bitter feelings (Genesis 50:15-21).

Where does this grace come from, this power to endure? Not merely from Bible study, not merely from prayer, not merely from fellowship with other disciples, but from personal victories gained in personal tests. We buy this power to endure by our own personal surrender and obedience to God's Word in the thick of real-life troubles. So valuable is it that Jesus likens it to gold: "I counsel thee to buy of me gold tried in the fire, that thou mayest be rich" (Revelation 3:18). With this Peter agrees: "That the trial of your faith, being much more precious than of gold that perisheth, though it be tried with fire, might be found unto praise and honor and glory at the appearing of Jesus Christ (1 Peter 1:7).

The power to endure is strictly a matter of spiritual conditioning, of what level of difficulties we become capable of handling. Every test we go through successfully conditions or prepares us to go through the next one. The more we take, the more we can take. Every strain we accept and bear in full submission to God, enlarges us and creates within us the ability to bear even greater adversities with equal ease. In this way, our tests are constantly taking us from one level of strength to a greater one. Every time we pass through another "Valley of Baca," or the place of trial, we "go from strength to strength—increasing in victorious power" (Psalms 84:5-7, AMP).

A good athletic trainer knows his athlete's endurance level and how much he can take without breaking. He constantly pushes him to the limits of his physical endurance, but never beyond. By repeated workouts at one level of exertion, the athlete gains strength to increase his output. As his strength increases, his endurance level rises. This new strength must then be put to the test. It must be exercised. The trainer, realizing this, changes his workout schedule to increase its difficulty. He requires more of him, making him work harder. He pushes him beyond his former limit of endurance, but not beyond his new one. And so, in this manner, a good trainer increases the power to endure in the athlete under his care.

Our God is the master trainer. He knows our personal capabilities perfectly—how much stress we can take, how much work we can turn out, how much confusion we can analyze and set in order, how much sorrow we can rise above, how long we can wait without becoming discouraged, etc. With the utmost care, He orders our personal tests according to our current abilities in Christ, never allowing the strain to be more than we can presently bear in Him: "God is faithful, who will not permit you to be tempted above that which ye are able, but will, with the temptation, also make the way to escape, that ye may be able to bear it" (1 Corinthians 10:13).

As we learn to overcome at one level of Christian experience, our spiritual strength is increasing. As we handle our God-given difficulties by carefully and consistently doing God's Word, our inner man is firming up. With each new victory, God toughens us: ". . . I will strengthen and harden you [to difficulties] . . ." (Isaiah 41:10, AMP). This new spiritual strength demands new testing. Therefore, our master trainer increases our workout schedule. He sends trials of greater severity and length. These new difficulties exercise our souls in new ways. We are constrained to work out our own salvation as never before. But, faithfully, God never pushes us beyond our current limit of endurance.

Frequently, it may seem as if our heavenly trainer has overworked us. We feel drained and pressed out of measure. But before we accuse the Lord of poor training, let's examine ourselves. Are we accepting every detail of our circumstances as from the Lord? "In all thy ways acknowledge me" (Proverbs 3:6). And are we abiding in close fellowship with the Lord daily and remembering to carefully obey His sanctifying commands?

Our trainer has made the conditions of spiritual success very plain. "If ye abide in me and my words abide in you . . ." (John 15:7-8). If after God increases His demands on us, we find ourselves out of it, it's probably because either we haven't yet fully accepted our circumstances as from Him or haven't carefully obeyed His Word in our new setting. We're fussing inwardly at our heavenly trainer and refusing to adapt ourselves to our new workout schedule. As soon as we yield, we'll realize that God never lays upon us anything we cannot endure as long as we accept, abide, and obey. With divine precision, He gradually increases the severity of our trials, causing them to begin and end at just the right moment: "Thus far shalt thou come, but no farther" (Job 38:11).

Disobedience reverses God's training process. It causes us to lose strength in our trials rather than gain it. If we rebel against today's tests, we're less able to meet tomorrow's difficulties. Our power to endure diminishes. The more trials we pass through in disobedience, the more spiritual power we lose. Before long, we begin to recognize this. It dawns upon us that we're failing miserably in the same situations we formerly overcame with ease. And Satan takes no time-outs. Mercilessly, methodically, frighteningly, the adversities of life continue to march right at us. Our adversary is playing to win and shooting to kill. His vexations are relentless, his onslaughts lethal. None of us can stand still spiritually. Our daily trials are constantly taking us up or down, into greater strength or weakness of character. From this perpetual process of trial there is no escape.

The power to endure is a relative thing. Our present circumstances seem easy or hard to us, depending solely upon what we have become accustomed to in our past experiences. When God's angels have protected you in a major hurricane, a gale doesn't frighten you. When the Lord has provided for you in a full-scale economic depression, a few months of recession seem easy. When by your

God you have endured reproach from your own family and close friends, it's a light thing when strangers speak evil of you. When you have waited on God for years before seeing the answers to your prayers materialize, it's nothing to wait a week or a month for His hand to move. When you have seen God provide when your income was completely cut off, a reduction in pay causes no panic. "His riches in glory" were sufficient before; they will be sufficient again (Philippians 4:19). Our past victories make our current tests less formidable. God did it for us in the past; if we continue to abide closely, He will do it again: "The Lord who delivered me out of the paw of the lion, and out of the paw of the bear, he will deliver me out of the hand of this Philistine" (1 Samuel 17:37).

Don't grumble or rebel against your trials. Your master trainer is utterly faithful and good. Realize what your trials are doing in you as you obey: "Thou hast enlarged me when I was in distress" (Psalms 4:1). Open your mouth and give the sacrifice of praise, "giving thanks to his name" (Hebrews 13:15). Allow the testing of your faith to enlarge you and increase you in the power to endure.

3

Made Strong Through Adversity

The righteous also shall hold on his way, and he that hath clean hands shall be stronger and stronger.

(Job 17:9)

In Job 17:1-9, Job describes his tribulation, prophesies the outcome he is expecting, and declares that his adversity will make him stronger.

Job says that he is:

Sick and ready to die: "My breath is corrupt, my days are extinct, the grave is ready for me."

Mocked and provoked continually: "Are there not mockers with me? And doth not mine eye continue in their provocation?"

Not vindicated by God: "Who is he who will strike hands with me?"

Misunderstood by his friends: "For thou hast hidden their heart from understanding."

15

A public laughingstock: "He hath made me
also a byword of the people; and I was as one
before whom men spit."

Of a sorrowful, hopeless outlook: "Mine eye
also is dim by reason of sorrow."

Yet in spite of all this trouble, Job declares, "The
righteous shall maintain his way, and he who has
clean hands will grow stronger" (17:9, Modern
Language Bible).

Job believes firmly that any sufferer who is truly
right with God and innocent of wrongdoing will
keep up his good living right in the midst of
unjustified affliction: "The righteous also shall hold
on his way . . . " (17:9).   Instead of being crushed
by adversity, he will be strengthened by it.   He
further states that when the full truth is made
known, good men, shocked, will rally behind him
and rise up to condemn the hypocrites who have
condemned him: "Upright men shall be astounded
at this, and the innocent shall stir up himself against
the hypocrite" (17:8).

What a mighty burst of faith!   Job begins his
speech with one foot in the grave, and ends it by
declaring that he fully expects to grow stronger and
stronger.   Faith lifted him from the grave of despair
to the rock of prophecy!   (See also Psalms 40:1-2;
Habakkuk 1:1-4; 3:17-19.)

Did Job's prophecy come true?   The last chapter
in the Book of Job describes "the end of the Lord"
(James 5:11).   When this blessed conclusion finally
came, Job was purer in heart, humbler in spirit,
clearer in spiritual vision, increased in knowledge,

confirmed in faith, closer to God, restored in relationships, and richer in blessings. In every way, then, he was stronger for having passed through his divinely arranged adversity in trust and obedience: "So the Lord blessed the latter end of Job more than his beginning" (Job 42:12).

In the Book of Genesis, Joseph's adversity is described: "Joseph is a fruitful bough, even a fruitful bough by a well, whose branches run over the wall. The archers have harassed him, and shot at him, and hated him; but his bow abode in strength, and the arms of his hands were made strong by the hands of the mighty God of Jacob" (Genesis 49:22-24). Oh, how Joseph was strengthened through adversity! At the time his envious brothers sold him into slavery, he was but the fair-skinned favorite son of Jacob: "Now Israel [Jacob] loved Joseph more than all his children, because he was the son of his old age" (Genesis 37:3).

But after God's adversity did its work upon Joseph, this boy became a man. And what a man he was! With God-given wisdom and skill, he counseled kings, administrated great works, handed down judgments, and foretold the future: "He made him lord of his house, and ruler of all his substance, to bind his princes at his pleasure, and teach his elders wisdom" (Psalms 105:21-22).

When Joseph's brothers were later reunited with him, they saw no untested youth on Egypt's throne. Joseph had become a full-fledged man of God— wise, strong, spiritual: "And Pharaoh said, Can we find such an one as this is, a man in whom the Spirit of God is?. . . there is none so discreet and wise . . . " (Genesis 41:38-39). The murderous persecution they

17

had instigated against their younger brother was intended to snuff him out. They hoped to terminate the "dreamer," as they called him, to quench his gift and silence his testimony forever. But instead, their very resistance made him strong and godly. Joseph's dreams and interpretations continued, the number of souls he helped increased greatly, and his testimony was established forever in the Holy Scriptures.

Nehemiah was also strengthened by the very adversity his enemies created to weaken him: "For they all made us afraid, saying, Their hands shall be weakened from the work, that it be not done. Now, therefore, O God, strengthen my hands" (Nehemiah 6:9). God heard Nehemiah's request to strengthen his hands and made this strong man of God even stronger. As Job had predicted, "The righteous also . . . shall be stronger and stronger." Rebuilding Jerusalem's wall was a tremendous task under even the best of conditions. But Nehemiah's circumstances were far from that. *In fact, they were the worst conditions conceivable.*

Consider what he was up against.

His enemies, the Samaritans, were strong, verbal, and very active. Throughout the reconstruction of the wall, they vexed Nehemiah daily. With each new day came yet another cross for him to bear, courtesy of the Samaritans.

They tried to discourage him by mocking the Jews' efforts: "What are these feeble Jews doing? Will they fortify themselves? . . . Will they finish in a day? Will they revive the stones out of the heaps of the rubbish, seeing they are burned?" (Nehemiah 4:2).

They planned a secret military assault on the city: "And conspired all of them together to come and to fight against Jerusalem" (4:8). They also sought to ambush the individual workers as they returned to their homes in the surrounding villages: "The Jews who dwelt by them . . . said . . . From all places where ye shall return unto us they will be upon you" (4:12).

They sought to waste his time in purposeless talk and repeatedly attempted to set him up for assassination: "That Sanballat . . . sent unto me, saying, Come, let us meet together in one of the villages in the plain of Ono. But they thought to do me mischief" (6:2).

They spread false reports about Nehemiah. One stated that he was planning to declare himself King of Judah and rebel openly against Persian authority: "Then sent Sanballat . . . an open letter . . . in which was written, It is reported among the nations, and Gashmu saith it, that thou and the Jews think to rebel; for which cause thou buildest the wall, that thou mayest be their king . . . now shall it be reported to the king according to these words" (6:5-9).

They even hired false prophets to try to trick Nehemiah into breaking God's Law, so that they might truthfully accuse him of wrongdoing: "And, lo, I perceived that God had not sent him, but that he pronounced this prophecy against me; for Tobiah and Sanballat had hired him. Therefore was he hired, that I should be afraid, and do so, and sin, and that they might have a matter for an evil report, that they might reproach me" (6:10-14).

In addition to these numerous difficulties from without, Nehemiah had much to contend with from within.

At first, the scene in Jerusalem was very depressing and the remnant quite discouraged: "The remnant . . . are in great affliction and reproach; the wall of Jerusalem also is broken down, and its gates are burned with fire" (Nehemiah 1:3).

Some of the wealthier citizens refused to lower themselves to do manual labor: "Their nobles put not their necks to the work of their Lord" (3:5).

The Jews who worked willingly suffered physical fatigue due to the sheer amount of work they had to do, and at times their morale dropped sharply: "And Judah said, 'The strength of the bearers of burdens is decayed' " (4:10).

Many of the workers also suffered from lack of food and great indebtedness: "Some also there were who said, 'We have mortgaged our lands, vineyards, and houses, that we might buy grain' " (5:3).

Worst of all, Nehemiah suffered treacherous betrayal. Many of his own people in Jerusalem were secretly informing Tobiah and Sanballat, his chief enemies, of all his plans and movements. Continually we read, "When Sanballat heard" (see verses 2:10, 19; 4:1, 7, 15; 6:1, 16). How did Sanballat hear? Tobiah "was by him" (4:3), passing along the information he was receiving from the "many letters" disloyal Jewish nobles were sending him throughout the reconstruction period: "Moreover, in those days the nobles of Judah sent many letters unto Tobiah . . . For there were many in Judah sworn unto him . . . and (they) uttered my words to him" (6:17-19).

In the face of such extreme opposition, we would
expect to read that Nehemiah eventually threw up
his hands, quit, and returned to Persia. But he did
not. Held in place by his faith, he "held on his way"
(Job 17:9). And with the help of God's sufficient
grace, he grew stronger and stronger as the days
went by. Miraculously, he finished rebuilding the
wall of Jerusalem in only fifty-two days. As his trial
comes to its close, we see Nehemiah fully established
in divine wisdom, strength, and authority.
Afterwards, he went on to lead the nation in
religious reform, initiating vital scriptural changes
that brought spiritual refreshment to the people of
God (Nehemiah 13:1-31).

Nehemiah's enemies, on the other hand, who
had worked so feverishly to weaken him, emerged
from the ordeal thoroughly undone. They were
shaken, silent, and bitterly discouraged: "So the wall
was finished . . . when all our enemies heard of this
. . . and saw these things, they were much cast down
in their own eyes; for they perceived that this work
was wrought by our God" (Nehemiah 6:15-16).

In *My Utmost For His Highest*, Oswald Chambers
states:

> God does not give us overcoming life:
> He gives us life as we overcome. The strain
> is the strength. If there is no strain, there
> is no strength. Are you asking God to give
> you life and liberty and joy? He cannot,
> unless you will accept the strain.
> Immediately you face the strain, you will
> get the strength. Overcome your own

timidity and take the step, and God will give
you to eat of the tree of life and you will get
nourishment.[1]

Job, Joseph, and Nehemiah were each made
strong through adversity. Apart from it, they could
never have become what God intended them to be.
God's method of making strong servants has never
changed. "For I am the Lord, I change not" (Malachi
3:6; Hebrews 13:8). He still sends trouble to make
us stronger and stronger. He wants iron in our
souls. He wants to strengthen our knees, firm up
our spiritual backbones, and thicken our skin. Why?
So that we might be ready for spiritual warfare. The
apostle Paul, who overcame many troubles, wrote,
"Be strong in the Lord, and in the power of his
might" (Ephesians 6:10). God wants us "fit for the
Master's use, and prepared unto every good work"
(2 Timothy 2:21).

The true work of God arouses fierce opposition
from the powers of the air and the souls they rule
over. Satan, demons, sinners, workers of iniquity,
carnal Christians, false prophets, all of these unite to
stamp out the soul who faithfully holds forth the
Word. For His work, therefore, God uses only those
who are strong, stable, and reliable in His sight: "Men
of might, and men of war fit for the battle"
(1 Chronicles 12:8).

---

[1]This material is taken from *My Utmost for His Highest* by
Oswald Chambers. Copyright © 1935 by Dodd Mead & Co.,
renewed © 1963 by the Oswald Chambers Publications Assn.,
Ltd., and is used by permission of Discovery House Publishers,
Grand Rapids, MI 49501. All rights reserved.

In these last and perilous days, as never before, the Lord needs strong Christian soldiers—tested, proven souls who have been made strong through adversity.

Will you be one?

4

Teaching and Testing

Therefore whosoever heareth these sayings of mine, and doeth them, I will liken him unto a wise man, which built his house upon a rock:

And the rain descended, and the floods came, and the winds blew, and beat upon that house; and it fell not: for it was founded upon a rock.

And every one that heareth these sayings of mine, and doeth them not, shall be likened unto a foolish man, which built his house upon the sand:

And the rain descended, and the floods came, and the winds blew, and beat upon that house; and it fell: and great was the fall of it.

(Matthew 7:24-27)

Most believers love being taught but hate being tested. We much prefer hearing to doing, listening to living, applauding to applying. But Jesus insists on testing us on every bit of spiritual truth we have heard. In the divine mind, teaching and testing go together, the two constant companions of the growing disciple.

In Christ, our lives are one unending cycle of teaching on the mountain and testing in the valley.

Every time we meditate in or study God's Word, or receive instruction from our teachers, we are, in a sense, on the mountain. We experience the Lord's instruction through His Word or His workers just as surely as His original disciples did in the days of His flesh: "He went up into a mountain: and when he was seated, his disciples came unto him. And he opened his mouth, and taught them, saying . . . " (Matthew 5:1-2). The mountain is the place where we are exposed to eternal truth. It's God's classroom.

The valley is the place where we must work out, or exercise, God's truth in practical living. It's God's laboratory. There, in personal experience, we discover the reality of what we have heard on the mountain. For every truth we receive on the mountain, God creates a corresponding test in the valley. He leads us into these appointed places of testing by the invisible working of His Spirit, exactly as He did His own Son: "And Jesus . . . was led by the Spirit into the wilderness, being forty days tested by the devil" (Luke 4:1-2). The very layout of the text in Jesus' sermon on the mountain confirms this.

The main body of the sermon is filled with teaching in which Jesus presents a wide range of spiritual truths that touch all areas of Christian thought and conduct (Matthew 5:1 - 7:23). Then, in the verses immediately following (7:24-27), He ends His sermon with a solemn prophetic warning of an approaching test. Thus, in the layout of the text, the Holy Spirit establishes a subtle pattern of teaching-testing. His implied message is this: As Jesus' warning of testing follows immediately after the main body of His teaching in the sermon on the mountain, so it is in our lives. *Our God-arranged tests follow hard after our teaching sessions, our personal sermons on the mountain. God teaches us, then tests us. We hear, then we must do. Every lecture in God's classroom is followed by experimentation in the lab of daily living.*

Jesus dealt in this manner with the original twelve disciples. He taught them on the mountain and then tested them in the valley. Their trials were not accidental, they always came down the lines of what they had been taught. God carefully tailored circumstances to give the disciples opportunities to do the very things in which Jesus had been instructing them.

Note carefully the connection between what Jesus taught the apostles in the sermon on the mountain and these tests that followed in their valley experiences.

Jesus taught the twelve to trust their heavenly Father for their daily bread (Matthew 6:11, 25-34). He then tested them by asking Philip where they could find food for the hungry multitude: "When Jesus then lifted up his eyes, and saw a great company come unto him, he saith unto Philip, Where shall we buy bread, that these may eat? And this he said to test him: for he himself knew what he would do" (John 6:5-6).

He instructed them to "Love your enemies, bless them that curse you, do good to them that hate you" (Matthew 5:44). He then used their long-standing religious enemies, the Samaritans, to test them. When some ungracious Samaritans refused to receive Jesus, James and John, forgetful of His teaching, promptly requested that they be allowed to call fire down upon them (Luke 9:54).

He told them, "Blessed are they who are persecuted for righteousness' sake," and "Let your light so shine before men, that they may see your good works, and glorify your Father which is in heaven" (Matthew 5:10, 16). He tested them at the High Priest's court. There Peter refused to suffer for righteousness' sake and vehemently denied knowing Him. Thus he hid his light under a bushel and did not glorify his Father in heaven (Matthew 26:69-75).

He taught them to persist in prayer: "Ask, and it shall be given you; seek, and ye shall find; knock, and it shall be opened unto you" (Matthew 7:7). He tested them at Gethsemane. There, instead of persisting in prayer, Peter, James, and John persisted in slumber (Matthew 26:36-46).

He charged them to "Resist not evil" (Matthew 5:39). He tested them when evil incarnate, Judas, came with a band of armed men to arrest Him. Peter immediately drew his sword and resisted the evildoers—exactly what Jesus had told him *not* to do (Matthew 26:47-54).

He exhorted them to "Have faith in God" (Mark 11:22). Then He tested them during the days immediately before and after His crucifixion. They proved to be slow of heart to believe all that He had spoken (Luke 24:25). Before His death, they disbelieved His repeated warnings of the crucifixion—after He rose, they doubted the eyewitnesses of His resurrection (Mark 16:9-14).

The Lord still deals with us today as He did the twelve. He teaches, then He tests. We hear, then we must do.

We are instructed on love and mercy. Shortly afterwards, we have an opportunity to forgive an offender, do good to an enemy, or help a stranger.

We undertake and complete a thorough study on faithfulness. The next week, we suffer a flood of self-depreciating, negative, unbelieving thoughts. Sore tempted to consider our work as futile, we almost give up faithfully executing our duties.

After hearing the word of faith, severe trouble besieges us. We are constrained to believe God and wait for His promised help.

After meditating on the words, "Ye cannot serve God and money," a lucrative job offer comes our way. But accepting it will mean leaving the position we know God has called us to.

These valley experiences are not accidents. They are the Lord's tests. They are the lab in which we put God's truth into practice. And they always follow hard after our teaching sessions. We hear, and not many days after, the opportunity arises for us to do exactly what we have heard.

The resurrected Christ chided two of His disciples for being "fools and slow of heart to believe" (Luke 24:25). Like them, we seem afflicted with chronic spiritual blindness. God puts His tests right in front of us but we don't recognize them. We're slow of heart to believe all He has told us, slow to believe that He has really created situations in our lives to see if we'll obey Him or not. We lack faith—that amazing spiritual insight that sees God in everyday occurrences. We're more dominated by carnal reasonings than by spiritual thoughts. Jesus taught that "even the very hairs of your head are all numbered" by our heavenly Father (Matthew 10:30). How then can anything touch our lives that He is not in, working all things toward some eternally good purpose?

> And they come unto thee as the people come, and they sit before thee as my people, and they hear thy words, but they will not do them ...
> And, lo, thou art unto them as a very lovely song of one that hath a pleasant voice, and can play well on an instrument; for they hear thy words, but they do them not.
> (Ezekiel 33:31-32)

God told Ezekiel that the people enjoyed hearing his preaching, as they would any other form of good, clean entertainment, but they were not doing what he was saying. In other words, they listen, but have no intention of obeying. They nod their heads, but harden their hearts. They shout "Amen," but it all ends there. They never closely examine themselves or make real changes in their thinking, talking, or doing. They constantly apply the Word to others, but rarely, if ever, to themselves.

Oswald Chambers referred to this class of believers as "enchanted, but unchanged." James calls them self-deceived "hearers only" (James 1:22). Paul had them in mind when he wrote, "Ever learning, but never able to come to the knowledge of the truth" (2 Timothy 3:7). Jesus likened them to fools, building houses on shifting sands: "And every one that heareth these sayings of mine, and doeth them not, shall be likened unto a foolish man, who built his house upon the sand . . . and it fell; and great was the fall of it" (Matthew 7:26-27). Does our present manner of living put us in or uncomfortably near this undesirable category?

In the days of His flesh, Jesus "began again to teach . . . and he taught them many things" (Mark 4:1-2). He's still teaching us many things today through many different channels: meditative Bible reading, Bible study, sermons, seminars, spiritual retreats, Christian books, publications, and taped messages. Yet many of us fail repeatedly when God tests us on the many things we have heard. It's not a matter of spiritual ignorance. We know what God says in His Word. Our problem is spiritual stupidity—that is, *rebellion.* We know, but foolishly refuse to do. We stubbornly hold back from applying the spiritual intelligence we have. We love to hear biblical truth expounded, to be inspired and blessed, but we're unwilling to execute in the test.

A. W. Tozer wrote:

> Christians habitually weep and pray over beautiful truth, only to draw back from that same truth when it comes to the difficult job of putting it into practice. . . . The mind can approve and the emotions enjoy while the will drags its feet and refuses to go along. . . . It appears that too many Christians want to enjoy the thrill of feeling right but are not willing to endure the inconvenience of being right."[1]

[1]*The Root of the Righteous* by A. W. Tozer, (© 1955, 1986 Lowell Tozer, published by Christian Publications, Camp Hill, PA)

Being taught is so painless, so enjoyable, so easy. We "hear the word, and immediately with joy receive it" (Matthew 13:20). But testing isn't fun. It's intense, demanding, costly. The instant God begins to test us, most of us get huffed and are "immediately . . . offended" (Matthew 13:21). The idea of having to prove ourselves to God repels us. We despise the humiliation of obedience. Therefore, many believers become skilled spiritual escape artists. They dodge, ignore, or openly flee from all foreseeable difficulties. Like Jonah, when the test lies to the east, they head west.

But we cannot long avoid the unavoidable. All who enjoy teachings on the mountain must endure trials in the valley. To attempt to evade our tests is to deny our Lord's teaching. He taught that rains, floods, and winds must eventually beat upon every Christian's life. Wise and foolish alike must experience the storm. All of God's students must take their final examinations. The wise Christian accepts this now and gets busy preparing for, and passing, His tests.

Why does the Lord persist in testing us? For at least three good reasons:

> To graft His Word into our souls;
> To enlarge our capacity for truth;
> To establish Christian character in us.

To Graft His Word

"Receive with meekness the engrafted [grafted] word, which is able to save your souls" (James 1:21).

By successful testing, God grafts His Word into our souls, making it real to us and in us. In a spiritual sense, the Word is made flesh in all who both hear and do (John 1:14). Truth is welded into the mettle of our character by the heat of trial. Thereafter, it remains a permanent part of our person.

When we hear but refuse to do, this grafting process cannot occur. We become hearers only and begin to deceive ourselves (James 1:22-25). Gradually, we lose touch with what we are really like. Hypocrisy sets in. The gap between our religion and our reality widens. If this continues, we end up a disgusting, deceived Pharisee, savorless salt, "thereafter good for nothing, but to be cast out, and to be trodden under foot of men" (Matthew 5:13). Why? Because we would not let God graft His Word into us.

The Word taught becomes the grafted Word only at the point that we bow and obey it. Truth acted is truth grafted. Disobeyed truth remains detached from the framework of our character. It is true, but it is not true *in us*. It is real, but not *in us*.

At the judgment, the Word will send away those in whom His Word is not grafted: "I never knew you; depart from me, ye that work iniquity" (Matthew 7:21-23).

To Enlarge Our Capacity for Truth

"Thou hast enlarged me when I was in distress" (Psalms 4:1). Successful testing enlarges our capacity for spiritual truth. When we hear and do, God rewards us by creating within us a new and enlarged ability to appreciate, understand, and apply divine truth. Suddenly, the Word is alive and full of meaning: "Then opened he their understanding, that they might understand the scriptures" (Luke 24:45).

Because of *doing* the Word, we are able to know more. Scriptures come together, questions are cleared up, doctrines become understandable: "If any man will do his will, he shall know of the doctrine . . ." (John 7:17). God gives sharper, clearer insight to the eyes of our understanding. The spiritual well within us becomes deeper and wider. We can now take in much more of what God has to say. We have ears to hear things we never heard before.

Why is this? Simply because we did what He taught us: "Whosoever heareth these sayings of mine, and doeth them . . ." (Matthew 7:24). We paid the price of obedience, implemented His instruction, and applied what we applauded. In short, we passed our tests. The enlarged mind is a valuable reward God yearns to give us: "That ye may be filled with the knowledge of his will in all wisdom and spiritual understanding" (Colossians 1:9).

To Establish Christian Character

"Therefore, whosoever heareth these sayings of mine, and doeth them, I will liken him unto a wise man, who built his house upon a rock" (Matthew 7:24). Successful testing establishes Christian character in us. Our character is the sum of our daily decisions and deeds in the actual conditions of life.

Our trials provide us with opportunities to choose and do that which is right in the Lord's sight. By righteous decisions and actions, we build righteous character. By tangible acts, we establish the fact that we do believe, we do fear God, we do follow our Lord. God, men, and angels look on and take note: "Now I know that thou fearest God, seeing thou hast not withheld thy son, thine only son from me" (Genesis 22:12). After such trials, none may protest or deny our faith. It is irrefutably proven by our acts.

Salvation comes "by grace . . . through faith" and is "the gift of God" (Ephesians 2:8-9). In it, God gives the divine *nature* to all that believe. But Christian *character* is entirely different. It's not a gift, but an attainment. It's the sum, not of God's decisions and actions, but of ours. It comes, not by grace, but by obedience. If we are ever to have it, we must build it ourselves. Note that Jesus said the wise man built his house: "*A* wise man, who built his house upon a rock." It was not built for him.

Now all Christians are building character, but not all are building Christian character. All Christians are building a *house*, but not all are building upon the *rock*. Those who hear and obey build an honorable Christian character on the rock. Those who hear Christ's sayings and *don't* obey them build a dishonorable character. By their actions in trial, they establish *unrighteous* character. Their wrong thoughts and errant choices produce evil deeds evident to God and man. These are the foolish virgins Jesus spoke of in Matthew 25:1-13. They are like the foolish man who builds his house of character on the sand (Matthew 7:26-27).

Strange as it may seem, among the vast number saved by the blood of the Lamb, there will be both honorable and dishonorable characters. God's great house, His kingdom, has in it both vessels unto honor and vessels unto dishonor: "But in a great house there are not only vessels of gold and of silver, but also of wood and of earth; and some to honor, and some to dishonor" (2 Timothy 2:20).

Daniel built his house of character upon the rock. He believed, obeyed, and overcame amid a variety of tests. Samson, however, built a dishonorable character. He preferred the sand. Repeatedly, he failed his tests. Every time God tested him, he simply would not obey. And every failed test established unrighteous character in him yet more. Finally, in Delilah's arms, his house fell apart.

Both Daniel and Samson were men who enjoyed right standing with God, but only one was honorable. Both were God's children, but only one was wise. Both were used of God, but only one pleased Him. Both built a house of character, but only one built Christian character. And it was *testing* that established the character of each.

Beloved, teaching and testing are the alternating rain and sunshine we need to become strong "trees of righteousness, the planting of the Lord, that he might be glorified" (Isaiah 61:3). When God tests you, give Him thanks. He is trying to graft His Word in your soul, enlarge your capacity for truth, and establish Christian character in you. So, "Whatsoever he saith unto you, do it" (John 2:5). Dig deep and build your house upon the rock.

5

Another Chance

*And the word of the Lord came unto Jonah
the second time, saying, Arise, go unto Nineveh.*

(Jonah 3:1-2)

Whenever we fail God in our various trials, if we
confess and repent, He faithfully forgives us and
restores our fellowship with Him: "If we confess our
sins, he is faithful and just to forgive us our sins, and
to cleanse us from all unrighteousness" (1 John 1:9).
But God doesn't stop there. He immediately
schedules another chance for us to obey. That is, He
providentially arranges another trial spiritually
similar to the one in which we just failed.

Why does God do this? To punish us further by
reminding us of our failures? No, His purpose is just
the opposite. He wants us to be able to forget them
completely. He provides us with another chance
that we might avenge our spiritual defeats and live
thereafter in the joy of overcoming rather than the

frustration of failure. He wants us to be more than forgiven—He wants us victorious.

God understands our deepest thoughts. He knows that even when we believe we're forgiven, the memories of our past failures tend to linger and vex us. Like David, we feel, "My sin is ever before me" (Psalms 51:3). In His mercy, therefore, God arranges another test for us so that these troublesome thoughts may be erased completely from our conscience and replaced with pleasant memories of trials overcome and victories won: "For by thee have I run through a troop; and by my God have I leaped over a wall" (Psalms 18:29). The blood gives us forgiveness, but only obedience under trial gives us the joy of overcoming. After redeeming our past defeats with fresh victories, we can close the book on our season of manifold trials and be filled with "joy unspeakable and full of glory" (1 Peter 1:6-8). The agitation of regret is gone, and the peace of accomplishment abides in its stead.

This is one of God's ways clearly taught in the Scriptures.

When God first ordered Jonah to preach to Nineveh, the prophet flatly rebelled. He went straight in the opposite direction: "But Jonah rose up to flee unto Tarshish from the presence of the Lord" (Jonah 1:3). Jonah's failure brought swift divine chastisement: "But the Lord sent out a great wind into the sea, and there was a mighty tempest." (1:4). After experiencing the terrifying storm and a three-day stay in the fish's belly, Jonah cried out with genuine repentance. God faithfully forgave him, delivered him, and restored his fellowship (2:1-10).

But God's dealings did not end there.

He promptly arranged for Jonah to be tested again, exactly as he had been tested before: "And the word of the Lord came unto Jonah the second time, saying, Arise, Go unto Nineveh" (3:1-2). In this second call, Jonah clearly recognized that he was being given another chance, and that he had a perfect opportunity to redeem his earlier failure. He quickly seized the opportunity: "So Jonah arose, and went unto Nineveh, according to the word of the Lord" (3:3). When he obeyed, God gave him miraculous success. Wicked Nineveh repented: "So the people of Nineveh believed God, and proclaimed a fast, and put on sackcloth, from the greatest of them even to the least of them" (3:5). Jonah's bitter memories of his previous failure were suddenly erased. The regret, frustration, and grief were gone. In their stead came the joy of overcoming and sweet memories of an amazing spiritual revival.

Under trial, Peter broke down and failed the Lord. He cursed and swore as he vehemently denied being one of Jesus' disciples. When Jesus turned and looked upon Peter, that one look inflicted more pain than a thousand lashes. Peter had failed his Lord grievously and he knew it. In the throes of a great personal defeat he wept his way through to repentance and confession: "And Peter went out, and wept bitterly" (Luke 22:62). Because he did, he was immediately restored to fellowship with God. So on the morning of the third day, we see the humbled apostle again leading his brethren (Luke 24:12). But although he was forgiven and restored, Peter was far from happy. His heart was still pained by the memory of his recent failure.

Mercifully, God did not leave him very long in this state. He promptly arranged another chance.

During the interim between the Lord's resurrection and His ascension, "Jesus showed himself again to the disciples at the Sea of Tiberias" (John 21:1). After fishing all night, the disciples were weary and hungry. So Jesus appeared, and kindly prepared and served them a breakfast of bread and fish (21:12-14). After they had eaten, Jesus turned to Peter in front of the others and asked him the same question three times: "Lovest thou me?" (21:15-17). Three times Peter responded, "Yea, Lord; thou knowest that I love thee," publicly confessing his loyalty to the Lord.

Why did Jesus ask these three identical questions? Because He was giving Peter another chance. It was Peter's opportunity to redeem himself. He had denied the Lord three times in public, and now he was being given three more opportunities to confess Him in public. His three confessions erased the bitter memories of his three previous denials. When Jesus ascended several days later, Peter was more than a forgiven man—he was victorious, joyful, and strong.

Let us be encouraged. If we fail God under trial, we need not succumb to despair. Defeat is not inevitable, nor is victory impossible. Like Jonah, let us look again to our merciful Lord for another chance: "Then I said, I am cast out of thy sight; yet I will look again toward thine holy temple" (Jonah 2:4).

Our next trial may be identical to the one we just failed, as it was with Jonah. Or it may be a test of the same spiritual quality—faith, mercy, courage, generosity, patience, forgiveness, forbearance, etc.— but set in different circumstances among different people, as it was with Peter. Another chance may come immediately after our failure, or it may come days or even weeks later. But it will surely come. God never misses a single detail.

Whenever our next opportunity comes, let us seize it. Let us trust where before we feared, give where before we held back, confess where before we denied, stand true where before we compromised, and press on where before we stopped short. And let us lay hold of the joy of victory where before we suffered the shame and frustration of defeat.

6

God Is Watching

And Othniel, the son of Kenaz, Caleb's younger brother, took it; and he gave him Achsah, his daughter, in marriage.

(Judges 1:13)

Don't underestimate the importance of the tests in which you presently struggle. If passed successfully, they may open doors for you in God that are exceedingly abundantly above anything you ever dreamed of: "Though thy beginning was small, yet thy latter end should greatly increase" (Job 8:7).

After Joshua's death, Israel began to possess fully the territory it had subjugated during his lifetime. The first tribe to take its land was Judah (Judges 1:1-3). In one of the first battles, Caleb offered the hand of his daughter, Achsah, in marriage to whoever successfully led Judah against the city of Kiriath-sepher, which was also called Debir. His nephew, Othniel, stepped forward and accepted his challenge. And with God's help, Othniel took the city.

Therefore, Caleb "gave him Achsah, his daughter, in marriage" (Judges 1:11-13).

By faith, Othniel wrought a victory and gained a reward. But more importantly, he won God's approval, for God had been watching the situation as it developed. He observed Othniel's courage, faith, and skill in action at Kiriath-sepher. After the battle was over, He knew He had Himself a good man in the son of Kenaz. While Othniel was rejoicing over his first earthly victory, something far better was happening in heaven above. God was writing Othniel's name down on His list of overcomers and reserving a bigger, better place for him in the days ahead.

Some years later, Israel sinned and came under bondage to Cushan-rishathaim, King of Mesopotamia. After eight years of his bitter oppression, the children of Israel cried unto the Lord for help. God then called upon Othniel to come forth and challenge the oppressor. Years earlier he had taken a city; now he would have the chance to deliver a nation (Judges 3:5-11).

In Othniel's experiences, we see one of God's ways. God gives His big assignments to those who have proven themselves in "the day of small things" (Zechariah 4:10). This principle is expressed in one of Jesus' parables: "His Lord said unto him, Well done, thou good and faithful servant; thou hast been faithful over a few things, I will make thee ruler over many things" (Matthew 25:21).

As military engagements go, Othniel's first victory at Kiriath-sepher was a relatively small thing. Kiriath-sepher was no imposing fortress. It did not compare with the heavily fortified capitals of Assyria, Babylon, or Egypt. Its name means "city of books and scribes." Many of its occupants were evidently harmless scribes—peaceful men of pen and paper, not fierce warriors of spear and sword. Its fall was insignificant in the eyes of secular historians. Neighboring kings probably didn't even discuss the battle over their evening meal. To them, it was a small thing. But it was a victory, nonetheless, and one that Othniel was glad to have. Sensational triumphs over mighty heathen nations would come later. For now, he was thankful to have taken a city, any city.

Othniel was obviously a humble man. Other men of war might have turned down Caleb's offer, opting to wait for a larger conflict, something more impressive, more newsworthy. Those with the pride of Naaman or Goliath may even have scoffed that Kiriath-sepher was beneath them. They were too important to waste their time on small things. But not Othniel. He took the little things seriously.

He realized that the size of a trial has nothing to do with the character qualities that God is testing and developing in that trial. Faithfulness is faithfulness, courage is courage, patience is patience, diligence is diligence, regardless of the apparent significance or insignificance (as people see it) of the situation in which we are being exercised. Jesus had this truth in mind when He said, "He that is faithful in that which is least is faithful also in much; and he that is unjust in the least is unjust also in much" (Luke 16:10).

The battle at Kiriath-sepher may not have commanded the attention of Palestine's kings, chiefs, and mighty men, but the eyes of the Lord watched Othniel's performance there with intense interest: "For who hath despised the day of small things? For they shall rejoice and shall see . . . they are the eyes of the Lord, which run to and fro through the whole earth" (Zechariah 4:10).

Othniel's later conflict with the King of Mesopotamia, however, was no small thing. For Israel, it was a crisis hour. The future of the chosen people was on the line. For Othniel, it was a great and effectual door, the opportunity of a lifetime. If he succeeded, his entire nation would go free. If he failed, their bitter yoke would remain and likely tighten. His adversary, Cushan-rishathaim, was as evil a king as you can imagine. His name means "doubly-wicked Cushan." And Mesopotamia's army was made up of proven, able warriors. Unlike the lesser battle at Kiriath-sepher, this was a frightful encounter with a wicked and formidable foe. But with God's Spirit strengthening, guiding, and keeping him, Othniel prevailed: "The Lord delivered Cushan-rishathaim, king of Mesopotamia, into his hand; and his hand prevailed against Cushan-rishathaim" (Judges 3:10).

This victory was in no wise insignificant, either before God or man. It both commanded attention and demanded recording. It was the fall of one nation and the rising again of another, not the defeat of a single, isolated city. It was a joyous emancipation from heathen domination for all Jews, an exodus from sorrow and despair. It renewed their personal faith and national hope in the God of Israel.

The rewards of the latter battle were also great. As the Psalmist wrote of the rewards of obedience to God's Word: "In keeping of them there is great reward" (Psalms 19:11). Israel received forty years of peace and freedom. Her enemies were silenced and God's honor was vindicated. Othniel was promoted to be the leader and judge of God's people. And as the first of Israel's judges, his name is honored to this day.

Friend, don't think lightly of your present trials. Your relatively small battles at *your* Kiriath-sepher may seem unimportant to you and go unnoticed by others, but they are not small. They are big, terrifically big. They will determine your future in God. God Himself is watching: "Thy Father, who seeth in secret" is right there where you are, in the thick of your day of small things.

Remember what is written:

> The eyes of the Lord are in every place, beholding the evil and the good.
>> (Proverbs 15:3)

> The eyes of the Lord are upon the righteous.
>> (Psalms 34:15)

> Thou God seest me.
>> (Genesis 16:13)

When God is watching, the smallest matters become immensely important. Nothing that holds His attention is insignificant.

Bear in mind that spiritual victories aren't always won in ways that appear victorious to the natural eye. Jesus won by losing, by letting evil men nail Him to a cross without cause. We may win our battles by letting others have their way, by not resisting mistreatment or demanding our rights. Spiritual strength at times appears to be weakness. We overcome by surrendering and accepting things as our heavenly Father has arranged them. We win our arguments by refusing to argue: "The servant of the Lord must not strive" (2 Timothy 2:24).

We move up in God by stepping down among men. We make progress by refusing to bull ahead. We gain strength by standing still in trust. Whatever the particulars of our trial may be, we may be sure of one thing: *Spiritual victory comes simply by obeying God*—"Whatsoever he saith unto you, do it" (John 2:5). God doesn't care how things look just now—whether we appear strong, weak, victorious, or defeated in the eyes of men—only that we trust and obey Him. That's how He measures victory. He knows how and when to make our victory apparent to us and to others.

Your part in the Lord's battles that are yet to come depends entirely on your present performance at your Kiriath-sepher. If you refuse to stir yourself up to courageous obedience, the heavenly watchman will see this and, with a heavy sigh, He will note your failure in His book. But if you, as Othniel, rise above the smaller challenges that surround you, God will know that He can count on you in the future. He will write your name on His list of overcomers and reserve for you a bigger, better place in His great master plan. And when the Church's crucial hour of deliverance comes, you will get His call: "Rise, he calleth thee" (Mark 10:49).

Be encouraged, overcomer. Today we take cities for God—tomorrow we conquer nations.

7

Rise Above It!

And he that overcometh . . .

(Revelation 2:26)

In our lives there are evil people who, as thorns in our flesh, vex us. There are also hindering circumstances that, as imposing mountains, block our way. Because of these, we experience painful, ongoing trials. Their continuing presence seems to prophesy endless misery, and we become almost certain they will remain forever to vex and hinder us. But they will not. When they have served their purpose, their presence will cease. When we rise above them, the Lord will remove them.

God is the great Circumstancer in our lives. He moves and shifts and rearranges the scenes in which we live. Constantly, His seasons blow over us: "He changeth the times and the seasons; He removeth . . . and He setteth up" (Daniel 2:21). Friends come and others leave. Our boss leaves and another takes his place. We move to a different city, take a new job, attend a new school, join a new fellowship. The situations and circumstances of our lives constantly change. Yet in the midst of these apparently haphazard changes, every detail of our lives remains completely under God's control. This unshakable confidence that God controls all (Romans 8:28) is the only foundation strong enough for the overcoming life. It's the spiritual bedrock upon which the overcomer builds.

God sends evil people (thorns) and hindering circumstances (mountains) our way for a distinct purpose. He uses them to develop the character of His Son in us. The divine objective is to reproduce the characteristics of Jesus Christ in ordinary people like you and me, to manifest the beauty of the Lord our God in us in this present ugly world, and to disperse the light of righteousness through us in the midst of our sin-darkened society.

> For it is God who worketh in you both to will and to do of his good pleasure.
>
> That ye may be blameless and harmless, children of God, without rebuke, in the midst of a crooked and perverse nation, among whom ye shine as lights in the world.
>
> (Philippians 2:13, 15)

It is for this reason that God sends His thorns and mountains into our lives. They are His means to His end in us—that we may be "conformed to the image of His Son" (Romans 8:29).

Christlikeness is synonymous with the fruit of the Spirit. To be conformed to the image of God's

Son is to have the Spirit's fruit present and growing within us. Jesus said, "In this is my Father glorified, that ye bear much fruit" (John 15:8). And to this the apostle Paul adds, "The fruit of the Spirit is love, joy, peace, long-suffering, gentleness, goodness, faith, meekness, self-control" (Galatians 5:22-23).

God wants Christ's love and gentleness made real in us. Therefore, He chastens and instructs us until we become patient and kind in the midst of long-suffering: "Love suffereth long, and is kind" (1 Corinthians 13:4). God also wants Christ's meekness and self-control to be found in us so that we remain submissive to Him and merciful toward our adversaries in the face of ongoing mistreatment. He longs for Christ's goodness to fill us so that our motives, desires, and goals become purified and we forsake all malicious intentions. He seeks to instill in us Christ's untouchable joy and undisturbable peace so that we cannot be irked by life's most insistent vexations. Above all, He wants us to possess overcoming faith and have steady, Christ-like confidence in Him when *everything but His Word* tells us that He is nowhere to be found. This sweeping transformation doesn't happen overnight. It comes *only* as the result of a sustained right reaction to the difficult people and situations God sends our way.

The instant we surrender our will to God and submit, acknowledging His hand in our adversity, we begin to grow in His purpose. He then begins to teach us how to overcome the difficulties, how to abide in Him while they remain intact, how to put off the old man and put on the new, and how to maintain a patient faith in His ultimate justice and reward.

When we realize that even that which is intended by Satan to tear us down has come from God to build us up, we take a new attitude toward our former dreads. We begin to think like someone who is more than a conqueror (Romans 8:37). Anxiety goes and joy rises from within. Our spirit comes again and we begin to enjoy life once more. What has happened? New understanding has brought with it fresh inspiration. Soon we rejoice over foes we formerly retreated from. Why? Because we see our enemies from a new viewpoint. God is using them to raise us up, to make us spiritually mature, to ripen the fruit of His Spirit in us. They mean evil against us, but God means it for our good (Genesis 50:20).

At this point, we are beginning to rise above the circumstantial muck by the superiority of spiritual-mindedness. We have taken the first important steps down the road that will eventually end in God's intervention and our personal deliverance.

After we have learned to walk in God's ways in minor trials, and our spiritual state is strong enough to handle it, God sends some of His master trials our way. They shock us with dismay. Our spiritual equilibrium is temporarily lost. We are knocked down, but not out: "Persecuted, but not forsaken; cast down, but not destroyed"(2 Corinthians 4:9).

Smitten and wounded in spirit, we feel overwhelmed: "For the enemy hath persecuted my soul; he hath smitten my life down to the ground . . .

Therefore is my spirit overwhelmed within me" (Psalms 143:3-4).

Our sense of justice is outraged. We can hardly believe what has happened. In despair we cry out to God and hold on for dear life. In such times we do well to survive: "Thou hast kept me alive" (Psalms 30:3).

Like Jacob, we cling to God until we regain our spiritual composure. Temporarily unable to advance, we take refuge in God, hold our ground, and endure: "Yea, in the shadow of thy wings will I make my refuge, until these calamities be passed by" (Psalms 57:1).

As we hold on, something wonderful begins to happen. The Spirit of Life from God re-enters us and our strength and confidence revive: "Wait on the Lord; be of good courage, and he shall strengthen thine heart" (Psalms 27:14). Being thus strengthened by our God, we stand to our feet and face again the thing that knocked us down.

What has happened? We have endured unto the end of our trial and the Lord has saved us from going under: "But he that shall endure unto the end, the same shall be saved [delivered]" (Matthew 24:13). We have advanced beyond our former spiritual limitations into a new, broader place of living: "He brought me forth also into a large place; he delivered me . . . " (Psalms 18:19). It was touch and go for a while, but by God's grace we've come through.

Now, exactly how do we overcome mean people?

There is a saying that we all know, *Kill them with kindness.* Although this may be practiced with a vindictive motive—sweet words used to convey bitter feelings, it nevertheless expresses perfectly how we must handle the evil people God sends to try us. By patience and kindness, we *de-thorn* our thorny adversaries. By our overcoming attitude, we bind the evil spirit that moves them. Obedience to our Master's teaching makes us spiritually untouchable. Because they sense they cannot get to us, our enemies are frustrated in their attempt to stumble us. This overcomes their mean spirit toward us. Their evil joy is quenched.

When they cannot make us fall, our enemies have no peace: "For they sleep not, except they have done mischief; and their sleep is taken away, unless they cause some to fall" (Proverbs 4:16). Yet even this gnawing dissatisfaction is the mercy of God. It's God's Spirit working on their consciences to bring them to the acknowledgment of the truth, that they may repent: "If God, perhaps, will give them repentance to the acknowledging of the truth" (2 Timothy 2:25).

By overcoming our adversaries we are doing them good, if they will but yield to God. Through our actions He is leading them to repentance: "The goodness of God leadeth thee to repentance" (Romans 2:4). As overcomers, rather than hurt our enemies, we liberate them by overcoming the mean spirit that dominates them: "That they may recover themselves out of the snare of the devil, who are taken captive by him at his will" (2 Timothy 2:26).

In so doing, we fulfill the weighty scriptural command, "Be not overcome by evil, but overcome evil with good" (Romans 12:21).

As we consistently overcome in this manner, God begins to intervene in our behalf. The pressure of His almighty hand bears down on our opposers. By our actions toward them, we have proven our obedience to God. Now the issue is entirely between them and God. Either repentance or removal inevitably follows, for it is a serious thing to oppose one of the least of God's little ones. The Master warned all who would listen:

> Whosoever shall offend one of these little ones who believe in me, it were better for him that a millstone were hanged about his neck, and that he were drowned in the depth of the sea.
>
> Woe unto the world because of offenses! For it must needs be that offenses come; but woe to that man by whom the offense cometh!"
>
> (Matthew 18:6-7)

It's an equally serious offense to do "despite unto the Spirit of Grace" (Hebrews 10:29)—to steadily refuse God's gracious attempts to turn our hearts toward Him. If our antagonists persistently refuse to allow *mercy* to lead them to repentance, *justice* will lead them to judgment. David's experiences with King Saul illustrate this perfectly.

Saul stood as a towering mountain, an apparently immovable obstruction before the anointed but severely-tested son of Jesse. This mountain had to either repent or be removed before David could build a highway of righteousness through the land. Through David's kindness, God gave Saul ample opportunity to repent. Twice David demonstrated the goodness of God to Saul by sparing his life when it was his to take. By his acts, David proved his submission before God and man. He rose above his mountain by demonstrating obedience, integrity, and compassion.

But in spite of David's kindness, Saul would not change. He continued to defame and persecute David. He admitted his sin on several occasions but never repented. His stubborn stand left God no alternative other than to remove him. Because Saul rejected mercy, justice took over. God intervened and moved the mountain out of David's way—permanently. Saul fell in battle against the Philistines: "And the battle went heavily against Saul, and the archers hit him . . . So Saul died" (1 Samuel 31:3, 6). Then David, as the new king, built a wide highway for God, His people, and righteousness—right where the mountain previously stood.

In the end, the Lord avenged David because he obediently refused to avenge himself: "Dearly beloved, avenge not yourselves but, rather, give place unto wrath; for it is written, Vengeance is mine; I will repay, saith the Lord" (Romans 12:19).

David never intended to harm Saul. All he wanted to do was obey and live. He aspired only to come into all that God had promised him. Yet his non-retaliatory actions brought on the Lord's intervention. God smote Saul, as he had Nabal earlier, because David's actions firmly established that he would not be moved by the spirit of vengeance: "And David said to Abishai, Destroy him not . . . As the Lord liveth, the Lord shall smite him; or his day shall come to die; or he shall descend into battle, and perish. The Lord forbid that I should stretch forth mine hand against the Lord's anointed" (1 Samuel 26:9-11).

God avenges only those who forsake the spirit of vengeance. He will not fight for those who still have the fight left in them. Consequently, David was genuinely grief-stricken at the death of Saul and Jonathan (2 Samuel 1:17-27). Nothing in him could rejoice.

Why did not God remove Saul years earlier? He gave David a sudden victory over Goliath. Could He not have constrained Saul to step aside quickly and make room for his anointed successor? Why did He allow those awful years of harassment? Why did He not step in much sooner than He did to end the conflict and bring David to Israel's throne?

Because God was using Saul as David's training ground. David practiced the forgiveness of God upon him. Because of David's spiritual attitude, the many evils that Saul did to David were but hurdles to leap over: "By my God have I leaped over a wall" (Psalms 18:29). Every time Saul wronged him, David would rise above the wrong by forgiving Saul in his heart and going on with God, thanking Him for the opportunity to learn how to overcome.

There were many such hurdles in the race set before David: Saul reneged on his promise to give his daughter, Merab, to David in marriage; he twice tried to kill him with his spear; he sent his servants to assassinate him; he forced him out of his job, his home, his marriage; he gave his wife, Michal, to another man in marriage; he slandered David's good name throughout Israel; and he hunted him for years in an attempt to physically extinguish his life. But David rose above each offense by simply obeying God's command to forgive and choosing to think spiritually instead of carnally. After years of this spiritual training, David became consistently spiritual in thought, word, and deed. He arrived at the finishing line. Then the hurdles were taken away and God promptly promoted him from the training ground to the throne room.

It's the same with us today.

The oppressors in our lives, the troublesome circumstances that we must endure, these all have a distinct purpose from the throne of God. They are not meaningless objects flung carelessly in our way, but divinely designed hurdles placed with the utmost care. We must learn to leap over them efficiently and effortlessly by obedience to God's Word. This will not happen suddenly or easily. It will take practice, practice, and more practice. It will require diligence, determination, and the willingness to suffer for the Lord's sake. *Will we pay the price?*

Remember, the hindering circumstances that seem to bar our way are neither accidental blockages nor man-made barriers—they are mountains formed and placed by the hand of our God. We must learn to rise up and tread upon them in the name of the Lord.

It is the character of Christ, the fruit of the Spirit, that our heavenly Father seeks to develop in us. Thorns, mountains, hurdles, these are but the instruments He uses. When His objective is achieved, He will lay down His instruments. When we have manifested the spirit of a conqueror towards *our* Sauls, God will relieve us of them. He will either bring them to repentance or remove them. They will either wither in willing surrender to God or be cut down by divine judgment (Psalms 37:1-2). But in either case, our trial will come to an end: "For surely there is an end, and thine expectation shall not be cut off" (Proverbs 23:18).

In the midst of our apparently endless trials, we may take comfort in this: *As soon as we rise above our trials, God will remove them.* Is this not sufficient incentive to overcome? May God stir us as never before to gird up the loins of our minds and rise above it!

Now rise up, said I, and get you over.

(Deuteronomy 2:13)

8

Take the Serpent by the Tail!

And the Lord said unto him, What is that in thine hand? And he said, A rod.

And he said, Cast it on the ground. And he cast it on the ground, and it became a serpent; and Moses fled from before it.

And the Lord said unto Moses, Put forth thine hand, and take it by the tail. And he put forth his hand and caught it, and it became a rod in his hand.

(Exodus 4:3-4)

In Exodus 4:1-9, God gives Moses final preparations and instructions before sending him on his great mission. In verses 1-5, He gives him power over all satanic power; in verses 6-8, power over all sickness; and in verse 9, power over the natural creation. And so, supernaturally empowered by God, Moses went forth to deliver God's people.

But verses 1-5 reveal that before Moses could withstand, confound, and defeat mighty Pharaoh, he had to get the victory over a much less formidable opponent—one little serpent. One little serpent which, at the time, had the upper hand. For Moses was scared of it and "fled from before it."

What odd behavior this was! Moses, the chosen deliverer, flee? Moses retreated from nothing and no one. Why did he flee? Evidently, he thought the serpent was something he could not deal with, something beyond his present capabilities. When mighty Moses fled, heaven must have been embarrassed. The devil had the deliverer on the run.

Then came God's challenge: "Put forth thine hand, and take it by the tail." God had seen Moses flee in fear. His command, therefore, was for Moses to reach out and conquer the serpent, to overcome the thing he feared. He had to square up and face the serpent and catch it by its tail, bringing it under his power. God was saying, in effect, "Go ahead Moses, don't be afraid of that serpent. I'm with you and will help you. Use the skills I've already taught you. Overcome the serpent, master him, defeat him. Don't allow a miserable little snake to keep you from fulfilling your great calling as the liberator of My people!"

God's challenge paid off. It awakened Moses' manly conscience and stirred his dormant courage. Immediately, and in faith, he acted: "And he put forth his hand, and caught it." Right where he had formerly come under, he came over. His panicky flight ceased and a controlled advance began—an advance that did not end until a string of mighty victories had been wrought, a nation delivered, and the name of God glorified for all time and eternity.

Moses' victory was much more than a minor triumph over a stray reptile. In the Scriptures, the serpent symbolizes satanic power (Revelation 20:2). This serpent Moses faced, however, was more than a mere symbol. The transformed rod became an actual embodiment of satanic power—the devil himself in snakeskin. Moses' opponent was the subtle but powerful creature who overthrew Adam in the garden (Genesis 3:1-6). Therefore, when he put forth his hand and caught it, his actions foreshadowed Christ's victory over Satan in the wilderness. As his Lord would later do (Luke 4:1-14), Moses met the evil one in a great test on holy ground and came away victorious. Now the previously embarrassing situation was completely reversed. The deliverer had the devil on the run. And heaven breathed a sigh of relief.

What followed Moses' victory? Immediately, the conquered serpent returned to being a rod in his hand. But it was no longer an ordinary rod, a simple shepherd's stick. It was now a noble scepter filled with the supernatural power of the living God. With that rod, Moses wrought miracles, judgments, and signs. With it, he humbled Pharaoh and confounded his magicians. With it, he invoked the plagues upon the Egyptians, opened and closed the Red Sea, obtained water from the rock, and controlled Israel's battle with the Amalekites. J. A. MacMillan wrote that Moses' rod symbolized "the authority of God committed to human hands."

It's clear then that *it was after Moses accepted God's challenge and took the serpent by the tail that God put power into his hands.*

There's a vital lesson here for us. God today has many men and women called after the order of Moses. They are deliverers in the making, souls who have the potential for being "strong in the Lord and in the power of His might" (Ephesians 6:10). Why? Because the nature of the Deliverer, Jesus Christ, is in them and His Spirit upon them. In this late hour, the Church needs deliverers desperately, every bit as much as Israel's exhausted slaves needed Moses. But before any of us can receive divine power to deliver men, we must first *take the serpent by the tail* as Moses did!

To us, the serpent represents satanic power in human flesh. Our contest is not with a wily viper, but with crafty, evil people. Satan works against committed disciples through every soul that refuses to yield wholly to Christ. They are taken captive by him at his will and used as his instruments of opposition against those who earnestly seek to follow the Lord wholly. This is the real explanation behind the patriarchs' persecution of Joseph, Saul's persecution of David, Judas' vexation of his fellow apostles, and Peninnah's ceaseless needling of Hannah: "And her adversary also provoked her relentlessly, to make her fret" (1 Samuel 1:6). Satan makes these human agents as bothersome as thorns and as deadly as snakes. They constantly create difficult situations for us to deal with, situations from which we, as Moses, have frequently fled.

Today God is challenging us to learn to handle the serpent whenever we encounter him in men: "And these signs shall follow those who believe; In my name . . . they shall take up serpents" (Mark 16:17-18).

When the devil seeks to hold us at bay through the workings of evildoers, we must outwit his strategy. To do this, we must remind ourselves constantly that "we wrestle not with flesh and blood, but . . . against spiritual wickedness" (Ephesians 6:12). Although people do wrestle against us, they are not the source of the opposition. They are but instruments in the hands of another. We must see through their actions and discern our real enemy behind them.

Ironically, the man who wrote, "We wrestle not with flesh and blood," found himself constantly grappling against human antagonists. Almost everywhere Paul ministered, Jews or Gentiles gathered together against him. Time and again he was falsely accused, hauled into court, beaten, whipped, stoned, or run out of town. Soon Paul went to the Lord with a petition of complaint, seeking relief from the overwhelming human opposition that dogged him (2 Corinthians 12:7-10). The Lord then revealed to him that his real enemy was not the people that were harassing him but a satanic spirit, a demon, that Satan appointed to buffet him with persecution and tribulation.

Why was Paul given a thorn in the flesh? For two reasons:

To keep him humble, because of the many spiritual revelations given him;

It was Satan's effort to stop the Word from going forth through his ministry.

The same serpent that confronted Adam, Moses, and Christ sought also to overthrow Paul. His goal was to have Paul become offended with God and thereby to prevent him from continuing to walk with Him, from sowing His Word, and from delivering both Jew and Gentile alike. After Paul understood this, he yielded and accepted his thorn in the flesh. There's no doubt it made it much easier for him to forgive his many offenders when he realized that a greater enemy was using them. Thus, by submission and obedience to Christ, Paul *took the serpent by the tail.* He overcame his real enemy. It was out of this enlightening personal experience that he penned his statement to us: "We wrestle not with flesh and blood, but . . . against spiritual wickedness."

With Paul's experience and Epistle in mind, it becomes much easier for us to forgive our offenders, refuse to be offended, and wait patiently for God's help. It also stirs us to realize that either we overcome the serpent or he cuts short our destiny.

After initially having fled from the serpent, Moses faced him and overcame. We must learn to do the same. Wherever we have backed down from our adversary, wherever we have appeased men merely to keep peace, we must now overrule our dread and stand firm. Wherever we have repeatedly succumbed to strife and anger, we must now overrule our stubborn self-will and be content to answer simply yes or no. Remember, wherever we have experienced repeated spiritual failures of any kind, Satan has had the upper hand—the serpent has made us flee. We must now determine to overrule the defeatism of unbelief and stand firm until we are victorious.

This will be no easy thing. We'll never take the serpent by the tail if we remain hesitant, half-hearted, double-minded. We must throw ourselves into this with an iron will. Where will this courageous resolve, this undefeatable faith, come from? From only one source—renewed faith in the promises of God's Word: "Faith cometh by hearing, and hearing by the Word of God" (Romans 10:17). Note carefully that it was when Moses heard God's voice, His Word, that he reversed his course: "And the Lord said unto Moses, Put forth thine hand, and take it by the tail . . . and he put forth his hand, and caught it." The Lord's voice strengthened him to face the serpent. It lifted him above the discouragement caused by his previous failure.

The same voice speaks to us today through the Scriptures, seeking to strengthen us to take our serpent by the tail. God wants to deliver us from fear, from the insidious uncertainty that inevitably arises in the wake of repeated spiritual failures. As we listen to His voice, our shakiness becomes sturdiness, our doubt, confidence. Listen to the voice of the Lord:

> Behold, I give unto you power to tread on serpents and scorpions, and over all the power of the enemy; and nothing shall by any means hurt you.
>
> (Luke 10:19)

> Greater is he that is in you, than he that is in the world.
>
> (1 John 4:4)

Stir up the gift of God, which is in thee.

For God hath not given us the spirit of fear, but of power, and of love, and of a sound mind.

(2 Timothy 1:6-7)

Fear thou not; for I am with thee. Be not dismayed; for I am thy God. I will strengthen thee; yea, I will help thee; yea, I will uphold thee with the right hand of my righteousness.

Behold, all they that were incensed against thee shall be ashamed and confounded.

(Isaiah 41:10-11)

Have not I commanded thee? Be strong and of good courage; be not afraid, neither be thou dismayed; for the Lord thy God is with thee wherever thou goest.

(Joshua 1:9)

We all know these Scriptures—now we must put them to use. Immediately and in faith we must act upon them. We must exercise the power we already have, the power of the Word, if we would qualify to receive the power of the Spirit (Luke 4:14).

To do this, we must change our naturally negative attitude into a scripturally positive one. This happens only as we say what we believe: "Let the redeemed of the Lord, say so" (Psalms 107:2). "If thou shalt confess with thy mouth . . . thou shalt be saved . . . with the mouth confession is made unto salvation" (Romans 10:9-10). With conviction, we must repeatedly confess every positive scriptural assertion we can think of, such as, "I can do all things through Christ, who strengtheneth me" (Philippians 4:13). And these confessions must be clearly in the present tense. That is, we can *now*! Not later on, when certain persons go or circumstances change. Now, right now, with things just as they are.

Through Christ who strengtheneth us *we can* take our serpent by the tail! We can traverse fields of testing filled with serpents and scorpions and all the power of the enemy and come forth without entanglement or injury. We can resist the devil without fretting at the people through whom he is working. We can divide the flesh from the spirit and forgive our offenders every time, knowing inwardly that we wrestle not with flesh and blood. We can withstand reproach and persecution and walk steadily forward with God when all hope that we should be saved is taken away (Acts 27:20). We can handle impossible people who try us to tears. We can master timidity and stand firm where formerly men's looks put us in fear. We can believe all things, bear all things, overcome all things. All we need is the stubborn human grit to accept God's challenge— His grace will supply the rest: "My grace is sufficient for thee" (2 Corinthians 12:9).

If Moses had not stopped fleeing from the serpent, he would never have received power. His destiny would have remained unfulfilled and his brethren undelivered. If we keep thinking and saying "we can't" overcome, we won't. And if we don't overcome, we'll receive no power. God will not commit His rod of authority into defeated hands.

And if we remain powerless, many needy Christians will go unhelped because of our personal failure. Is that the way we want it to be?

Today—this moment—*take your serpent by the tail!*

9

Determination

And they who went ahead rebuked him, that he should hold his peace; but he cried so much the more, Thou Son of David, have mercy on me.

(Luke 18:39)

Surprisingly, Jesus' disciples sometimes misunderstood, criticized, and actually opposed other believers who were moving in true faith and by the leading of the Spirit of God. This strange resistance, however, was God's way of forcing the seekers to exercise their determination.

Determination is persistence in the face of prevailing opposition. It's steadfastness, tenacity, grit. It's an indefatigable resolve to do God's will, a sturdy refusal to quit, based upon the conviction of the Spirit within. Godly determination is a mark of spiritual maturity. Maturity has been defined as, "Perseverance, the ability to sweat out a project or a situation in spite of heavy opposition and discouraging setbacks."

The Scriptures set forth several clear examples of this mature, determined attitude and of the unusual opposition that at times arises from Christian sources.

As blind Bartimaeus sought help from Jesus, the Lord's disciples opposed him: "And they who went ahead rebuked him, that he should hold his peace" (Luke 18:39). But their opposition only fueled his determination. He "cried so much the more" until he caught the Master's attention: "And Jesus stood, and commanded him to be brought unto him" (18:40). If Bartimaeus had not been a determined man, he would never have gotten through to Jesus.

When the Syrophenician woman came to Jesus (Matthew 15:21-28), what was the apostles' immediate reaction? Did they praise God? Were they blessed and thankful that a woman of great faith had come to pay a visit—a visit that would help her daughter, honor God, and become a shining example of faith to henceforth bless all Christendom? No—exasperated by her requests, they came to Jesus and begged Him to send her away: "And his disciples came and besought him, saying, Send her away; for she crieth after us" (15:23). Yet despite the rude treatment, the woman persisted and finally prevailed.

When Mary of Bethany broke her alabaster box of precious ointment and honored the Lord by anointing His head (Mark 14:3-9), did the apostles rejoice? Did they commend Mary for her great devotion to Jesus? No—rather than give support, they joined Judas in criticizing her. They said her sacrifice was a foolish, uneconomical waste: "And there were some that had indignation within themselves, and said, Why was this waste of the ointment made? For it might have been sold for more than three hundred denarii and have been given to the poor. And they murmured against her" (14:4-5). But their reproach didn't stop Mary. She continued to minister to the Lord.

When Paul set his face like a flint to go to Jerusalem (Acts 21:8-14), did his brethren encourage him to pursue this path that God put in his heart? Did they bolster his faith by telling him that God would see him through, no matter how difficult his journey? Did they assure him that Christian sufferings lead to eternal glory? No—they begged him feverishly *not* to go to Jerusalem. Luke writes, "And when we heard these things, both we, and they of that place, besought him not to go up to Jerusalem" (21:12). No doubt they shook their heads in disbelief as Paul held fast his course: "What mean ye to weep and to break mine heart? For I am ready, not to be bound only but also to die at Jerusalem for the name of the Lord Jesus" (21:13). Only after testing his resolve to the limit did they cease trying to turn him back: "And when he would not be persuaded, we ceased, saying, The will of the Lord be done" (21:14).

In all these examples, the determined seekers did not allow their misguided brethren to weaken their clear sense of purpose. They pressed on. Bartimaeus kept calling out for Jesus until He responded. The Syrophenician woman kept approaching Jesus until she received assurance that her daughter would be delivered. Mary of Bethany continued to anoint Jesus while the apostles murmured. And Paul kept journeying toward Jerusalem despite the strenuous objections of his fellow Christians.

In Miletus, Paul expressed perfectly the spirit of godly determination: "And now, behold, I go bound in the spirit unto Jerusalem, not knowing the things that shall befall me there, Except that the Holy Spirit witnesseth in every city, saying that bonds and afflictions await me. But none of these things move me" (Acts 20:22-24). Unwittingly, he spoke for all determined disciples everywhere. Their prevailing attitude is also, "None of these things move me."

> I have set the Lord always before me; because he is at my right hand, I shall not be moved.
>
> (Psalms 16:8)

> I said, I shall never be moved.
>
> (Psalms 30:6)

> God is in the midst of her; she shall not be moved.
>
> (Psalms 46:5)

> [God] is my defense; I shall not be moved.
>
> (Psalms 62:6)

> That no man should be moved by these afflictions, for ye yourselves know that we are appointed to these things.
>
> (1 Thessalonians 3:3)

Opposition is but a stage God builds in the life of the Christian, upon which he shows forth his determination before God and men: "Work out your own salvation" (Philippians 2:12). How can we exercise determination when all conditions are favorable and all bystanders supportive? Something must come against us. We must have some adversity. There can be no victory without an opponent, no prize without a contest. We cannot become overcomers without having something or someone to overcome. That's why God permits opposition to confront us. Therefore, to God's determined ones, *opposition is opportunity.*

Our determination shines brightest when circumstances are the darkest. It's blackest midnight and all hope that we should be saved is gone. Discouraging evidence abounds on every side. Friends turn away and other Christians lose faith and question us. One part of us would love to quit. But something in us says, "Don't do it. Hold steady, Christian," for deep down in our hearts the unfailing seed, God's Word, has been planted. We have His promise concerning the confounding problems at hand. Therefore, there is but one thing to do. We must press through all the opposition and get at what God has for us: "The kingdom of God is preached, and every man presseth into it" (Luke 16:16). This is the true spirit of determination. And God loves it!

The Lord's special approval awaits every determined disciple. As Job held up under Satan's vicious assault, God voiced His approval before Satan: "Hast thou considered my servant, Job, that there is none like him in the earth, . . . still he holdeth fast his integrity, although thou movedst me against him, to destroy him without cause" (Job 2:3). To the Syrophenician woman, Jesus said, "O woman, great is thy faith" (Matthew 15:28). Of Mary, He said, "Verily I say unto you, Wherever this gospel shall be preached throughout the whole world, this also that she hath done shall be spoken of, for a memorial of her" (Mark 14:9).

Could any honor bestowed by men begin to compare with this special divine commendation? What could be greater than the public praise of the Son of God? Determined disciples bring honor to the cause of Christ, and for that cause Christ honors them: "Them who honor me I will honor" (1 Samuel 2:30). In due season, their ears shall hear the blessed words, "Friend, go up higher" (Luke 14:10), and "Well done, thou good and faithful servant" (Matthew 25:21, 23).

Why do our Christian friends at times resist us in the way of the Lord? One of several reasons may account for this.

> The Christians in question may be disobedient to the Lord themselves. Disobedient souls constantly oppose obedient ones. Their lives are headed in completely opposite directions: "He that is not with me is against me" (Matthew 12:30). Hence, collisions occur frequently.
>
> They may have been stumbled spiritually, offended by some unfortunate occurrence in their walk with God. When we lose our

confidence in God, we inevitably render evil counsel. We advise tempted brethren to lean on the arm of flesh. The disillusioned Christian disagrees with the optimism of those who still follow the heavenly vision and reasons with them to turn back from their spiritual quest.

Our opposing friends may be envious of our zeal. Lukewarm Christians despise serious disciples, yet envy their devotion. When envy enters, the closest friends are instantly set at odds. The sweetest fellowship soon becomes the bitterest enmity: "And Saul became David's enemy continually" (1 Samuel 18:29). Christians with an evil eye want to throw cold water on our fervency and put out our devotional fire.

They may be false Christians. The Scriptures warn us plainly about false prophets, workers of iniquity, angels of light, and wolves in sheep's clothing: "False brethren . . . who came in secretly to spy out our liberty which we have in Christ Jesus, that they might bring us into bondage" (Galatians 2:4-5). As there was a mixed multitude in Israel, so there is in the Church. Some possess real Christianity; others only profess it: "For some have not the [true] knowledge of God" (1 Corinthians 15:34).

They may be true Christians under the influence of a false doctrine—sons and daughters of liberty presently bound by the erroneous commandments of men. Their false beliefs may cause them to oppose the stand we have taken. Or they may have odd, private scruples, strange notions, or unscriptural religious standards that we do not measure up to. So they write us off and count us among the heathen: "And when they saw some of his disciples eat bread with defiled, that is to say, with unwashed, hands, they found fault . . . holding the tradition of the elders" (Mark 7:2-3).

They may be relatively new converts and thus unable to understand the spiritual matters with which we grapple. Hence, they may find fault with us in ignorance, not understanding the deeper things of walking with God: "I obtained mercy, because I did it ignorantly in unbelief" (1 Timothy 1:13).

Or they may be good, faithful Christians whom the Lord has simply smitten with temporary spiritual blindness to test us. He may have shut their eyes to the things He is revealing to us just to see if we will press on with determination when our Christian friends fail to stand with us: "God left him, to test him, that he might know all that was in his heart" (2 Chronicles 32:31).

Have you put your hand to the plow and encountered surprisingly stiff opposition from, of all sources, *brothers and sisters in Christ?* Have some of God's called ones—the very children of the kingdom—misunderstood and misjudged you? Are they criticizing you for your sacrifices, telling you to hold your peace, or forbidding you to continue seeking God's help? Are they trying to discourage and dissuade you from the path the Holy Spirit has plainly led you to take?

Don't faint. Joseph, Moses, and David were all opposed by their *brethren* at first, only to be beloved and supported by them afterward. They had to press through their opposition and lay hold of the purpose for which God called them. So be of good cheer, you're in good company: "For in the like manner did their fathers unto the prophets" (Luke 6:22-23). Go forward with what God has told you to do. Doubt not the Spirit's leading: "Whatsoever he saith unto you, do it" (John 2:5). The opposition confronting you is God's call for your determination to come forth. It's your stage. Now act out the part of the determined disciple: "But none of these things move me" (Acts 20:24). Let none of these things move *you*.

> But I follow after . . .
>
> I press toward the mark . . .
>
> Let us, therefore, as many as be perfect, be thus minded . . .
>
> (Philippians 3:12, 14-15)

10

God's Sanding Process

But let patience have her perfect work, that
ye may be perfect and entire, lacking nothing.

(James 1:2-4)

Have you ever noticed how God uses the faults
of others to rid us of our own faults?

Fine wood furniture must endure a great amount
of sanding. All the rough places—the nicks, burrs,
and splinters—must be sanded until they are
perfectly smooth, unnoticed by the eye and unfelt by
the hand. Only then is the furniture ready for the
finishing process, the merchant's store, and the
buyer's home.

God wants to do the same thing with every
Christian. He seeks to make us fine furnishings in
His heavenly home: "A vessel unto honor"
(2 Timothy 2:21). To do this, He must rid us of our
chronic character flaws. He must bring us to
spiritual maturity, or perfection. We will never be

a vessel unto honor if we allow rough places of untouched carnality to remain in our characters. They must go. To accomplish this end, God sends His sanders into our lives.

God's sanders are people with obvious personality faults. They are impatient people, mean people, lazy people, stupid people, inconsiderate people, irresponsible people, rebellious people, strange people—personalities that go against the grain of our personality. God deliberately places these abrasive souls near us. He wants them to come in contact with us daily. They must rub against us as sandpaper rubs against unfinished wood furniture. One by one, all our faults, weaknesses, and bad attitudes must go from us, even as all the nicks, burrs, and splinters must go from the wood. That is, if we aspire to be a vessel unto honor in the Father's house.

When we first encounter these offensive folks, most of us rebel. These sandpaper types rub us wrong. They grate, annoy, and vex. They nearly drive us crazy. Complaints begin to pour out of us: "Why do I have to deal with this person?"

In our distress, we turn to prayer. Just maybe we can pray them out of our lives: "Lord, please send this man, this woman to another city. Liberate me, set me free. Don't let the wicked oppress me anymore!" But our impassioned pleas receive no response. Heaven is silent.

Then we fix our attention on our sanders' faults. If we can just get God to change them, our sorrows will cease. So we pray fervently for their deliverance: "Lord, these people are so mean, so hard, so unkind. I've never run into anyone like them before. Please deliver them, save them. They must be helped." Still no answer comes from above—and no divine intervention occurs below.

Slowly, we begin to realize that God is not going to remove these coarse folks. At least, not for the time being. Why? Because He Himself has sent them: "This thing is from me" (1 Kings 12:24). While we were fixing our eyes on their faults, God was fixing His attention on our faults. While we were longing for them to change, God was longing for us to change. While we were praying that their faults would cease, He was hoping we would confess and forsake *our sinful reactions* to them. Suddenly, we come into the light and begin to understand God's sanding process.

God uses the chronic personality faults of His sanders to give us the opportunity to acknowledge and rid ourselves of our chronic faulty reactions. If we rebel, if we refuse to obey His Word, we will remain unfinished vessels, imperfect and unfit for the Master's use. But if we yield and obey God's Word in our relations with our sanders, God will rub away our imperfections. Our faulty reactions will cease. We will become spiritually mature, consistent, finished.

God's sanding process works like this:

Case One: The Lord exposes you to those who openly do evil. Why? In order to give you an opportunity to "fret not thyself because of evildoers" (Psalms 37:1). Your evildoers' evil doings are not the object of God's dealings. He will deal with your evildoers—but later on, not now. At present, He seeks to sand away your fretfulness, your angry reaction to their evil doings.

Case two: You find yourself working for a demanding, inconsiderate boss. "Why me, Lord?" you ask. Because God wants to use him to sand away your slothfulness, your disorganization, your inefficiency. He wants to grind down your destructive tendency to excuse yourself. He's being tough with you so you will become tough on yourself. If you continue to indulge yourself, you will be of no value to the Chief Executive Officer of heaven. The instant you become tough on yourself, your job becomes easy.

Case three: You live or work with someone given to strife. Everything you say, they twist and argue over: "My soul hath long dwelt with him that hateth peace. I am for peace; but when I speak, they are for war" (Psalms 120:6-7). Daily the temptation to enter into strife is present. Your carnal nature lusts to have the last word. What is God doing? He is trying to sand away your contentiousness. He knows all about the strife you constantly face. It's the opportunity He's given you to not strive back: "Strive not about words to no profit, but to the subverting of the hearers" (2 Timothy 2:14). He wants to establish you in His grace, to perfect your self-control.

Case four: Your spouse is inconsiderate. Your wishes, and at times your needs, are deliberately ignored. And God does absolutely nothing about it. Why? Because before He begins dealing with your mate, He wants to deal with you. You are the one He seeks to sanctify wholly. He wants to sand away your selfishness, your willfulness, your stubborn insistence on having your way. Sometimes, the very fault we see so clearly in our spouse is the thing God wants to rid us of.

Case five: At church your Christian brethren always look to you to take the responsibilities, make the decisions, do the work, and see that things get done properly. Meanwhile, they help as little as they can. Their apathy and irresponsibility are irritatingly evident. Your heavenly Father knows all about this. Yet He temporarily allows it to remain for your spiritual growth. They mean it against you for evil, but He means it to you for good (Genesis 50:20). God is using their irresponsibility to rub away your irresponsibility. And to sand away that subtle self-pity that arises when others put things off on you. Let the buck stop with you. Let God purge you. Forgive those who should help, but don't. Accept the duties you know the Lord would have you assume. Fulfill them faithfully "as to the Lord, and not unto men" (Colossians 3:23), and you'll grow strong.

Case six: Your children disobey you constantly. You have made, announced, and enforced the rules, yet your olive plants still fail to submit. Daily their rebelliousness rises up to challenge you. God is deeply concerned about rebellious children—there's no doubt about that. But He's even more concerned about rebellious parents. He'll help you learn to bring your children under control, but first He wants to use them to sand away your rebellious reaction to them: "Be not thou rebellious like that rebellious house" (Ezekiel 2:8). Rebellious parents cannot raise submissive children. Therefore, you are God's primary objective—your children are His secondary objective. When you begin to let patience have her perfect work in your dealings with your children, God will begin to make them respond to your authority. When you obey God, they will obey you. The more you bring yourself under God's authority, the more your children will come under your authority: "For I am a man under authority, having soldiers under me" (Matthew 8:9).

In these and many other ways, God seeks to sand away our faults. He wants to raise our spiritual characters to a new level, to conform us to the image of His Son. He seeks fine, finished vessels for permanent placement in His great house. Therefore, He will not stop sanding until all our character faults have been worn away, until we are perfect and complete, lacking nothing. Every burr, every nick, every splinter must be removed, "that ye may be blameless and harmless" (Philippians 2:15), "that ye may stand perfect and complete in all the will of God" (Colossians 4:12).

Let God finish His sanding process in you: "Let us go on unto perfection" (Hebrews 6:1). Stop complaining about the faults in those around you. Face your own faults. Yield entirely to God and obey His Word.

You *do* want to be one of God's fine furnishings, don't you?

> But in a great house there are not only vessels of gold and of silver, but also of wood and of earth; and some to honor, and some to dishonor.
>
> If a man, therefore, purge himself from these, he shall be a vessel unto honor, sanctified, and fit for the master's use, and prepared unto every good work.
>
> (2 Timothy 2:20-21)

11

At Your Right Hand

And he showed me Joshua the high priest standing before the angel of the Lord, and Satan standing at his right hand to resist him.

(Zechariah 3:1)

The high priest, Joshua, was opposed by Satan, who stood at his right hand. There was no escape from the enemy. He was right there by the side of God's servant, continuously trying him.

This scriptural portrait teaches us an important spiritual lesson: *Every day God tests us and Satan tries us through those who are nearest us, even at our right hand.*

God is seeking mature disciples He can approve for service, saints whose obedience in fiery trials renders them worthy in His sight. He therefore tests His people daily, searching for overcomers: "Study and be eager and do your utmost to present yourself to God approved (tested by trial), a workman who

has no cause to be ashamed" (2 Timothy 2:15, AMP),
"that ye may be accounted worthy" (Luke 21:36).

Wise Christians seek to win God's full approval:

> Wherefore, we labor that, whether present or
> absent, we may be accepted of him.
>
> (2 Corinthians 5:9)

> Ye have received of us how ye ought to walk
> and to please God.
>
> (1 Thessalonians 4:1)

> We . . . do those things that are pleasing in
> his sight.
>
> (1 John 3:22)

Satan wants to break up our fellowship with
God. He exerts relentless pressure on committed
disciples, hoping the difficulty of our way will cause
us to become offended with our Lord: "When
affliction or trouble or persecution comes on account
of the Word, at once he is caused to stumble—he is
repelled and begins to distrust and desert Him
whom he ought to trust and obey, and he falls
away" (Matthew 13:21, AMP). All the persecution,
tribulation, vexation, and irritation is sent to make
us so discouraged that we quit. Satan's goal is that
we "curse God and die" spiritually (Job 2:9)—that
is, stop believing, obeying, serving, loving, hoping,
and living in union with God.

So the test is on. Satan is pressing and God is
testing. Behind everything the devil does against us

stands God, hoping we will overcome and keep the word of His patience: "Because thou hast kept the word of my patience, I also will keep thee from the hour of temptation which shall come upon all the world to try them that dwell upon the earth" (Revelation 3:10).

To test us, God must use those we come in contact with daily. This fact is so simple it's easily overlooked. How could He test our faith, patience, and love with those *not* present? People afar off pose no trial for us. Distance makes even our worst enemies seem friendlier than they are. It's the difficult people at our right hand who try our patience to the limit. They grate our souls to the bone. The home, office, workplace, school, church—these are the vital testing grounds where God seeks to make us real in obedience to His Word. Our *daily companions* are the ones through whom God works—spouses, parents, children, business associates, fellow workers, schoolmates, friends, fellow believers. Much of the unprovoked meanness and irritability we encounter from them arises solely because they are around us daily. Somewhere else, they would be peaceful, lovable souls. Around us, they are thorns, snakes, and scorpions.

Here is the explanation behind this. To be a servant of God's will, our stubborn self-will must be broken. To break our self-will, God must cross it and we must yield. To cross it, He must have others insist on and get their way. Not our will, but theirs is done. Not once, but many times we are overruled, outvoted, left out, or ignored. Although painful, this is good for us spiritually, if we understand and yield. For God is using them to destroy the thing that would destroy us. He is breaking the arrogant demands of our self life. When we see His purpose at work behind our opposers and yield, His will is done. Our self-will is broken. We are ready then to serve His will: "I delight to do thy will, O my God" (Psalms 40:8).

To stand strong in the evil day, we must learn to "be not overcome by evil, but overcome evil with good" (Romans 12:21). To overcome evil with good, we must have some evil to overcome. Some evil nearby—even at our "right hand," like Joshua. For this reason, God often permits the evil one to take our closest companions captive: "Taken captive by him at his will (2 Timothy 2:26). The spirit of the prince of this world comes upon them and moves them. For no apparent reason, they are gripped by bad moods, evil tempers, nervous rushes, and general irritability. When that happens, we overcome the spirit that has come over them by carefully obeying God's Word.

We put into practice words such as these:

Strive not about words to no profit.

(2 Timothy 2:14)

Forgive, if ye have ought against any.

(Mark 11:25)

Resist not evil.

(Matthew 5:39)

Count it all joy when ye fall into various trials.
>> (James 1:2)

Let patience have her perfect work.
>> (James 1:4)

Be not afraid, neither be thou dismayed.
>> (Joshua 1:9)

Speaking the truth in love.
>> (Ephesians 4:15)

In every thing give thanks.
>> (1 Thessalonians 5:18)

Offer the sacrifice of praise to God continually, that is, the fruit of our lips giving thanks to his name.
>> (Hebrews 13:15)

As we obey God's Word, we prevail over the spirit of the enemy. We overcome evil. God's will is done and we are strengthened to stand and serve Him in the evil day.

The faults of those at our right hand grind on us methodically. At times we are so vexed we feel like shouting. We feel enclosed in a tiny room without windows or doors. The pressure builds. But as we hold fast to the simple, sanctifying Word, this circumstantial pressure becomes the very means of our growth in grace: "Thou hast enlarged me when I was in distress" (Psalms 4:1). It hastens our spiritual maturity, our character transformation into the image of Christ: "Conformed to the image of his Son" (Romans 8:28-29).

How could the Lord perfect love and mercy in us unless He permitted hasty, hardhearted people to rub elbows with us daily, even hourly? Their gracelessness is our opportunity to develop Jesus' graciousness in our mortal flesh.

How can the fruit of long-suffering be real in us unless we endure long-lasting personality defects in people we live or work with?

This spiritual pressure also determines our potential value to God as a workman that needeth not to be ashamed. The diamond is one of the most valuable substances known to man. As the diamond is formed under great, long-lasting pressure, so God's most valuable saints are formed amid protracted, pressurized trials: "Until Christ be formed in you" (Galatians 4:19). God wants to make us valuable jewels in His eternal kingdom: "And the foundations of the wall of the city were garnished with all manner of precious stones" (Revelation 21:19). The pressure is His way of making us strong and valuable.

In all of this, our adversary the devil has his own plans. He hopes to draw us out of our place of abiding in Jesus, spoil our disposition, halt our discipleship, and prevent our usefulness to God. We must not be naive. Through the resistance of those at our right hand, Satan himself seeks to defeat us. He entices us, as he did Adam, to disobey God's

Words—*any* of God's Words. And if we do, and fail to recover ourselves by confession and repentance, like Adam, we fall.

This spiritual wrestling is at times intense. If we don't judge ourselves carefully, we may develop great resentment, a "root of bitterness," towards those God is using to train us (Hebrews 12:15). This is easy to do. We estimate them to be the worst individuals that ever drew breath—more vile than Ahab, Jezebel, Judas, and Herod combined. We forget they are only instruments of the enemy and begin thinking they are the enemy. Now angels they're not, but neither are they the devil. They're only his agents. They're ordinary flesh and blood folks just like us.

Our fight is not with the instrument but with the one using it: "We wrestle not with flesh and blood, but against . . . spiritual wickedness" (Ephesians 6:12). To avoid being overcome by evil, we must remember this often. Very often. Sometimes minute by minute. We must set our minds to see them from the spiritual viewpoint: "For to be carnally minded is death, but to be spiritually minded is life and peace" (Romans 8:6). And we must live in constant surrender to the command, "Fret not thyself because of evildoers" (Psalms 37:1-11).

We must also remember Peter. Before Peter was sanctified, he was used both as God's instrument and Satan's within a short span of time. God revealed to him that Jesus was His Son, prompting the utterance, "Thou art the Christ, the Son of the living God" (Matthew 16:16). Jesus promptly commended Peter, saying, "Blessed art thou Simon

Bar-jona; for flesh and blood hath not revealed it unto thee, but my Father, who is in heaven" (16:17). But only moments later, Peter was inspired by the enemy. When Jesus first revealed His determination to go to the Cross (16:21), Peter openly resisted Him: "Be it far from thee, Lord; this shall not be unto thee" (16:22). Jesus then rebuked Peter, calling his spirit satanic: "Get thee behind me, Satan: thou art an offense unto me; for thou savorest not the things of God, but those that are of men" (16:23). So we see that Peter was susceptible to both God and Satan. Both used him as an instrument. Both spoke through him. And Jesus could discern every time who was working through Peter.

Peter, so typically human, represents us. If we don't watch ourselves closely, we too may be used by the enemy as well as God. This should give us some understanding for those who vex us daily. We must remember that it's the spirit of the enemy that moves upon them so frequently. Like Peter, they may be normal one minute and satanically-inspired the next. We must believe this and pray often for discernment. Then, like our Lord, we will learn to distinguish between divine and diabolical inspiration.

Besides, we don't know if our vexing companions may repent and go on to become fruitful servants of God: "If God, perhaps, will give them repentance to the acknowledging of the truth, and that they may recover themselves out of the snare of the devil" (2 Timothy 2:24-26). On more than one occasion, Peter stood at Christ's right hand to resist Him: "Thou shalt never wash my feet" (John 13:8). But look what he became—a pillar in the Church (Galatians 2:9). The fact that someone is Satan's agent to vex us doesn't mean there is no hope for them.

Surprisingly, God stands back and lets the devil do his infernal worst. For years He allowed Peninnah to reproach Hannah for her barrenness: "Her adversary also provoked her relentlessly, to make her fret" (1 Samuel 1:6). Why? Doesn't He care? Of course! It's because He does care for us that He permits evildoers to abide at our right hand. He wants to raise us up. He wants us to be all that we can be in Him. He seeks to mature us spiritually that we may dwell closer to Him than ever before. He wants us to have a deeper peace and joy than anything we have known. He wants to open the eyes of our understanding to a thousand truths we never understood. He seeks to approve us for our share of the work of the ministry so that we might know both the joys and rewards of fruitful Christian service. And testing, at times fiery testing, is the only road that can take us to this promised land of Christian blessedness. So, in love, God permits the persisting adversity. True, the enemy means his relentless assault against us for evil—but the Lord means it for good. If we believe this, it will take the sting out of every thorn in the flesh that vexes us.

When the enemy stands at your right hand pressing you, remember this: *Behind everything is God.* Back of every evil you suffer stands the devil, but back of the devil stands God. In love He seeks for men and women He can bless, approve, use, promote, and reward: "And I sought for a man among them" (Ezekiel 22:30). In this late and perilous hour, God needs proven servants for His work. Let Him make you one!

12

Merciless Criticism

And they watched him . . . that they might accuse him.

(Mark 3:2)

Jesus lived under the constant scrutiny of His enemies. Everywhere He went the Scribes and Pharisees were anxiously awaiting Him, looking for apparent imperfections in the perfect one. Humanly speaking, this put our Lord under terrific pressure. Yet He accepted this pressure, came to expect it, and graciously overcame His critics time and time again. He was the consummate overcomer.

He even sought to help His antagonists. While they busied themselves seeking an indictment against Him, Jesus voluntarily shared with them glorious divine truths. By teaching His critics, He loved His enemies, as He taught us to do: "The bloodthirsty hate the upright, but the just seek his soul" (Proverbs 29:10). Jesus repeatedly perceived the wickedness of His detractors, confounded them with His unapproachably wise speech, and then gave them a goodly portion of truth which, if heeded, would have saved them from their errors (Matthew 22:15-46).

John wrote, "As He is, so are we in this world" (1 John 4:17). As "they watched him . . . that they might accuse him," so they will watch us that they might find fault. If we belong to Him, we will receive the same suspicious stares that our Lord endured: "The servant is not greater than his lord. If they have persecuted me, they will also persecute you" (John 15:20). The enemies of the Lord (religious and non-religious) are incurably preoccupied with the true children of the kingdom. With insatiable curiosity, they constantly examine us: "And Saul eyed David, from that day and forward" (1 Samuel 18:9). One slip of the tongue, one false step, one obvious sin, one contradiction of our professed faith in God's promises, and our slip-up is quickly noticed and enthusiastically recorded against us. Not once in a while, mind you, but every time. Our enemy-critics have no mercy. At least, none for us. They cast out of their mouths cruel comments like a flood, hoping to carry us away: "Consider mine enemies; for . . . they hate me with cruel hatred" (Psalms 25:19). Such is the nature of merciless criticism.

But we must learn to not complain. God Himself is behind this severe spiritual scrutiny. He intends to use it for our good: "Ye thought evil against me; but God meant it unto good" (Genesis 50:20). If we fight against our critics, strife will consume us: "If ye bite and devour one another, take heed that ye be not consumed one of another" (Galatians 5:15). Resentment and bitterness will fill our veins. Our relationship to God will sour and our usefulness will cease. If we accept the pressure of reproach as coming from our Father, however, we'll grow from it: "But the more they afflicted them, the more they multiplied and grew" (Exodus 1:12).

That's what David did. When bitterly reviled by Shimei, David acknowledged God's permission, His sovereign allowance of what was happening: "So let him curse, because the Lord hath said unto him, Curse David . . . Let him alone, and let him curse; for the Lord hath bidden him" (2 Samuel 16:10-11). David realized that Shimei's caustic comments, though inspired from below, were ordained from above. He learned to accept such evil as from the Lord.

Are we really willing to "resist not evil"? (Matthew 5:39). Are we submissive enough to God to neither fear nor rebel against "the reproach of men"? (Isaiah 51:7). If so, the "fruit of the Spirit" will grow rapidly in our lives (Galatians 5:22-23). Our non-retaliatory attitude, based not in cowardice, but in true spiritual-mindedness, will deeply please and glorify God: "If ye be reproached for the name of Christ, happy are ye; for the Spirit of glory and of God resteth upon you; on their part he is evil spoken of, but on your part he is glorified" (1 Peter 4:14). Such an attitude, if persisted in, will convert our critics. Like the Jordan before Joshua, their flood of bitter words will be cut off: "For so is the will of God, that with well-doing ye may put to silence the ignorance of foolish men" (1 Peter 2:15).

Merciless criticism is a thorn in the flesh. Paul listed reproaches (criticisms) as one of the thorns Satan used to constantly vex him. At first he tried to pray away his critics: "For this thing I besought the Lord thrice, that it might depart from me. And he said unto me, My grace is sufficient for thee . . . Therefore, I take pleasure in infirmities, in reproaches, in necessities, in persecutions, in distresses for Christ's sake" (2 Corinthians 12:8-10). But the Lord's answer, when accepted, gave Paul a new outlook on his old enemies. Because Paul understood that His thorn in the flesh was for his spiritual welfare, to keep him from being puffed up (12:7), he restfully accepted his disturbing opposition: "Most gladly, therefore, will I rather glory in . . . reproaches" (12:9a). This humble attitude kept Him strong in spirit: "That the power of Christ may rest upon me" (12:9b). When he submitted to the difficult will of God, he was victoriously superior to his enemies: "For when I am weak, then am I strong" (12:10).

We must do the same. As long as we stay right with the Lord, our critics will keep talking. They must. *Periodic reproach is the unavoidable price of growing spiritual life.* We must, therefore, keep ourselves strong to bear this criticism. We must also be quick to discern any part of it that may be justifiable: "For what glory is it if, when ye are buffeted for your faults, ye shall take it patiently?" (1 Peter 2:20). Unjustified reproach is the cross—by it we are counted worthy of the kingdom and our Lord is honored. Justified reproach is the chastening of the Lord—by it we are painfully reminded of things we should have already dealt with and our Lord is put to grief: "One of themselves . . . said, The Cretans are always liars, evil beasts, lazy gluttons. This testimony is true. Wherefore, rebuke them sharply, that they may be sound in the faith" (Titus 1:12-13).

Every serious disciple must wake up and face the music. The spirit of this world does not like the true Christian one little bit. Neither do carnal Christians care for fully-committed disciples. The Philistines and King Saul had one thing in common—they both sought David's downfall. All who are worldly (Christian and non-Christian) are secretly glad to find fault with those who are becoming spiritual: "But as then he that was born after the flesh persecuted him that was born after the Spirit, even so it is now" (Galatians 4:29). We must therefore be doubly sure that we do not give our enemies any rightful charge against us. God's honor is at stake in our individual lives. We must not give His enemies any evidence to use against Him: "By this deed thou hast given great occasion to the enemies of the Lord to blaspheme" (2 Samuel 12:14).

Also, we have told others that we have a close relationship with the Lord. Should not our living agree with the things we preach and testify? And besides, we should want to know of any faults that hold us back from being what God would have us to be. Do we want to end up common hypocrites or uncommon overcomers? We mustn't complain when the world notes discrepancies between our spiritual talk and our unspiritual walk. They may not mean to, but our faithful faultfinders are helping us.

Merciless criticism, therefore, is a good evil—it's an adverse thing that God uses to achieve His good end in our souls: "I make peace, and create evil; I, the Lord, do all these things" (Isaiah 45:7). Criticism makes us watch our step. It forces us to conquer our carelessness, to constantly gird up the loins of our mind lest we fail our God. It keeps us stirred up to be at our best for the sake of the Name, lest some Shimei should be found justified in his rash charges against us. Thus, in His infinite wisdom, God uses even the pressure of persecution for our good. The severe scrutiny of our enemies is, in a sense, our heavenly Father's rod driving us into the reality of sanctification. As it is written, "all things work together for good" and "this is the will of God, even your sanctification," that we might be found in that day "conformed to the image of His son" (Romans 8:28-29; 1 Thessalonians 4:3).

13

Refreshing Spirituality

It may be that the Lord will look on mine affliction, and that the Lord will requite me good for his cursing this day.

(2 Samuel 16:12)

When David was forced to abandon his throne, it was a dark time for him (2 Samuel 15-18). His own son, Absalom, had slandered him and stolen the hearts of the people: "The conspiracy was strong; for the people increased continually with Absalom" (15:12). Absalom possessed David's city, his palace, and his throne. Rejected, dishonored, and wounded in spirit, David returned to the wilderness—the same wilderness where he had taken refuge from Saul long ago. The chances of his returning to power seemed small. Everyone was fascinated with the young, ambitious Absalom. The new leader's popularity was growing by the hour. It seemed that David had had his day, that God was finished with him. As David pondered the situation, his heart must have been heavy with grief. To say things looked bad is an understatement. Things could not have looked worse.

At this low point, a man named Shimei came along to add insult to injury—literally (2 Samuel 16:5-14). He bitterly reviled David and challenged him to retaliate: "He came forth, and cursed continuously as he came. And he cast stones at David, and at all the servants of King David . . . And thus said Shimei when he cursed, Come out, come out, thou bloody man, and thou worthless fellow" (16:5-7).

Shimei's words, "Come out, come out," have profound meaning. Through them, Satan was speaking, seeking to draw David out of abiding in the Lord. He succeeded in doing this in the beginning with Adam. God told Adam not to eat of the tree of the knowledge of good and evil. Satan planned his strategy, therefore, with one end in view—to entice Adam to eat of *that* tree. Why? Because such an act would be rebellion against God and break Adam's relationship with his Creator. Then God's holy justice would have to be satisfied. Adam would have to be put out of beautiful, fruitful Eden, his place of blessing. This is precisely what happened. Adam disobeyed God's Word; by that act, he came out from abiding in his relationship with God; and he was immediately expelled from his place of blessing: "Therefore the Lord God sent him forth from the garden of Eden . . . so he drove out the man" (Genesis 3:23-24).

Shimei didn't realize the significance of the words he was speaking. He was just a bitter, angry Benjamite. Evidently, he had never gotten over David becoming king years earlier. In his demented mind, Saul was still the better man. He considered David's present distress to be God's judgment upon him for having rebelled against Saul. He mistook Absalom's diabolical insurrection for God's divine intervention: "The Lord hath returned upon thee all the blood of the house of Saul, in whose stead thou hast reigned; and the Lord hath delivered the kingdom into the hand of Absalom, thy son; and, behold, thou art taken in thy mischief, because thou art a bloody man" (2 Samuel 16:8).

Satan, who inspired Shimei, knew well the profound implications of his challenge. He longed for David to put himself out of the will of God. Through Shimei's words, Satan was saying, "David, come over here and retaliate. Resist the adversity that has come upon you. Don't submit to it as from God. Fight it. Come out of that attitude of acceptance you have and stir yourself up to contention. Throw off God's yoke and rebel."

But David refused to go the way of Adam. He had a better idea, a refreshingly spiritual idea born of the Spirit of God. Here is how his idea came into being.

After hearing Shimei's words, Abishai, David's less-spiritual associate, advised David to retaliate: "Then said Abishai . . . Let me go over, I pray thee, and take off his head" (16:9). But David knew better. God's law was written on his heart. If he fought for himself, God would not fight for him. If he avenged himself, God would not avenge him: "Say not thou, I will recompense evil; but wait on the Lord, and he shall save thee" (Proverbs 20:22)—"Dearly beloved, avenge not yourselves but, rather, give place unto wrath; for it is written, Vengeance is mine; I will repay, saith the Lord" (Romans 12:19). If David took matters into his own hands he would take them out of God's hands. Realizing this, he put his trust in the Lord and awaited His intervention.

David's experience with Nabal was also imbedded in his soul. Surely, he could still hear Abigail's wise counsel ringing in his ears. She had pleaded with him not to avenge himself with his own hand (1 Samuel 25:26). If he had, it would have been a grief and offense of heart to him all his remaining days. He had yielded to her counsel before and God honored it. So he decided to do the same thing again with Shimei. He would keep his weapons idle and let God sling Shimei out of *His* sling, even as He had Nabal.

With this in his heart, David turned to Abishai and ordered him to put away his sword: "Let him alone" (16:11).

Immediately after David spoke to Abishai, God enlightened him. Like a flash of light, Truth shined a bright divine thought into his heavy heart. And David said, "It may be that the Lord will look on mine affliction, and that the Lord will requite me good for his cursing this day" (16:12). Why did God give him this burst of spontaneous spiritual understanding? Because his restraint of Abishai was an act of obedience to God. The moment he finalized his obedience by saying, "Let him alone," the Holy Spirit spoke to his heart, and out came the revelation, "*It may be . . .*"

David's revelation was simply this: Special blessings would be his because of Shimei's vicious reproach. If Shimei hadn't cursed him, God wouldn't have granted any special blessings. But now, because of Shimei's verbal attack, additional divine favors would come David's way. God would turn his cursings into blessings: "The Lord thy God turned the curse into a blessing unto thee" (Deuteronomy 23:5). He would make "all things work together for good" for David (Romans 8:28).

David had faith that *uncommon opposition overcome brings uncommon rewards to the overcomer.* The measure of extra blessing is equal to the measure of extra persecution endured. Joseph endured extraordinary persecution: "The archers have harassed him, and shot at him, and hated him" (Genesis 49:23). Because of this, God gave him extraordinary blessings. Jacob prophesied, "The blessings of thy father have prevailed above the blessings of my progenitors unto the utmost bound of the everlasting hills: they shall be on the head of Joseph, and on the crown of the head of him that was separate from his brethren" (Genesis 49:26). So David acquiesced in his present distress because he believed it would ultimately bring him extra blessings.

This spiritual understanding inspired David to overcome. It comforted, strengthened, and cheered him. It kept him: "Understanding shall keep thee" (Proverbs 2:11). It gave him spiritual rest—the "power to hold himself calm" in the midst of disturbing adversity (Psalms 94:13, AMP). Consequently, he kept his cool in a very hot situation.

Though he never said it, David may well have thought to himself, "Shimei, I am glad you came out to curse me today. Your denunciation is a blessing, your condemnation a lift in spirit. Because of this evil you have done, God will surely bless me with blessings that would not have been mine unless you had come out against me. Thank you for what you have done for me: 'Ye thought evil against me; but God meant it unto good'" (Genesis 50:20).

As the scene closes, Shimei is vexed and thoroughly discontented: "Shimei went along on the hillside opposite him, and cursed as he went, and threw stones at him, and cast dust" (2 Samuel 16:13). He was an emotional wreck. Naturally, we would expect him to be as relieved and peaceful as a spent volcano. But not so. He was more wretched than ever. Why? Because evil people do not rest "unless they cause some to fall" (Proverbs 4:16). Shimei had not succeeded in stumbling David. The evil attitudes he held remained unsatisfied. Shimei's sin could find no whipping boy. Therefore, he had no rest: "There is no peace, saith my God, to the wicked" (Isaiah 57:21).

On the other hand, David and his men were thoroughly refreshed by the whole experience. They "refreshed themselves there" (16:14). How could this be? We would expect him to be bristling with anger after the flood of false accusations that had just been directed at him. But he was supernaturally held by God's peace: "The peace of God, that passeth all understanding" (Philippians 4:7). Why? Because he chose to be spiritually minded toward his affliction: "For to be carnally minded is death, but to be spiritually minded is life and peace" (Romans 8:6). He acknowledged the heavenly arranger behind his earthly afflicter: "The Lord hath said unto him, Curse David . . . the Lord hath bidden him" (16:10-11). And he chose to not avenge himself. Therefore, his spiritual attitude gave him life and peace. He was physically rejuvenated and a strong, clear peace settled in on his mind.

Shortly after this incident, Absalom was killed and David returned to Jerusalem. On his way, whom should he run into but *Shimei* (2 Samuel 19:16-23). Shimei was the first man to greet David after he crossed over the Jordan. He humbly fell before David, confessed how evil he had been, and asked for forgiveness. David must have been glad then that he had not executed him. His faith was confirmed. As he had hoped, God had done His work on Shimei. Shimei's conscience was the scene of a great miracle. David's bitterest enemy was suddenly broken in repentance. David wrote: "It is God who avengeth me, and subdueth the peoples under me" (Psalms 18:47).

Fellow disciple, have you been falsely accused of late by some Shimei type? Have you been grossly misrepresented, mercilessly reviled, and challenged to fight back? Let David's experience save you from a great snare. Choose to be spiritually-minded toward your afflicter. Don't allow your enemy to draw you out of your place of safety and blessing. If you allow yourself to be drawn into carnal retaliation, either in desire or act, your peace will spread its wings and fly away. Recompense to no one evil for evil, accusation for accusation, insult for insult. If you must respond, be strong, brief, and to the point: "Let your communication be Yea, yea; Nay, nay" (Matthew 5:37a). But don't be drawn into strife or vengeance, "for whatever is more than these cometh of evil" (5:37b).

Remember David's revelation and take courage. If you had never been reproached for righteousness' sake, there would be no reward. Because of it, fresh rewards are reserved for you:

> Blessed are ye, when men shall hate you, and when they shall separate you from their company, and shall reproach you, and cast out your name as evil, for the Son of man's sake.
>
> Rejoice ye in that day, and leap for joy; for, behold, your reward is great in heaven. . . .
>
> (Luke 6:22-23)

> For this is thankworthy, if a man for conscience toward God endure grief, suffering wrongfully.
>
> . . . but if, when ye do well and suffer for it, ye take it patiently, this is acceptable with God.
>
> (1 Peter 2:19-20)

So simply do what David did. Fear not, stand still, and let God fight for you. And be very careful to obey His Word yourself, for, "when a man's ways please the Lord, He maketh even his enemies to be at peace with him" (Proverbs 16:7).

If you'll hold your peace and continue to believe and obey God, you'll have calm in the midst of chaos. Nothing will be able to get to you. You'll abide as strong and immovable as Mount Zion, "which cannot be removed, but abideth forever" (Psalms 125:1)—"steadfast, unmovable, always abounding in the work of the Lord" (1 Corinthians 15:58). And it may be, yea, it *shall* be, that God shall bless you with special blessings because of the special reproach that has been directed at you. Believe this.

As cold waters reinvigorate a thirsty soul, David's refreshingly spiritual attitude will cool the chaffed spirit of every falsely accused child of God.

14

When Relief Is on the Way

Then the disciples, every man according to his ability, determined to send relief unto the brethren who dwelt in Judea;

Which also they did, and sent it to the elders by the hands of Barnabas and Saul.

Now about that time Herod, the king, stretched forth his hands to vex certain of the Church.

(Acts 11:29-30; 12:1)

Unusually strong vexation is often a sign of approaching blessing from God. Acts 11:27-12:4 demonstrates this truth.

The brethren in Judea were in trouble. A great famine was approaching and many of them were already living on the edge of poverty. So God, in His mercy, sent the prophet Agabus to the large and growing church in Antioch. Through prophecy, he advised the saints there of the coming plight of their Judean brethren: "And in these days came prophets from Jerusalem unto Antioch. And there stood up one of them, named Agabus, and signified by the Spirit that there should be great famine throughout all the world, which came to pass in the days of Claudius Caesar" (11:27-28).

The Christians in Antioch were deeply moved by this timely prophecy and felt compelled to help the Judean church in a material way: "Then the disciples, every man according to his ability, determined to send relief unto the brethren who dwelt in Judea. Which also they did, and sent it to the elders by the hands of Barnabas and Saul" (11:29-30). Thus, in a time of great need, God did not forget His faithful ones in Judea. Relief was on its way.

But while Saul and Barnabas were en route, the brethren in Judea came under a direct and brutal attack from Satan: "Now about that time Herod, the king, stretched forth his hands to vex certain of the Church" (12:1). "About that time" means, in practical terms, "meanwhile." So we see that *as God's relief was on its way, Satan, through Herod, was vexing those who were about to receive it*. The key element here is timing. Paul's mission of mercy and Herod's vicious attack occurred *simultaneously*.

The Judean church had no idea that relief was coming. All they knew was that Satan had come in on them "like a flood" (Isaiah 59:19). Without warning, Herod broke out and "killed James, the brother of John, with the sword. And because he saw it pleased the Jews, he proceeded further to take Peter also . . . And when he had apprehended him, he put him in prison, and delivered him to four quaternions of soldiers to keep him; intending after Easter to bring him forth to the people" (Acts 12:2-4).

The apostle James is suddenly arrested and executed. Peter, the Church's strongest leader, is taken into custody and held for execution. It looked like the end for him, too. Why the heavy spiritual attack? Out of nowhere and for no apparent reason, Herod erupted in fury against the brethren. They had dwelt in Jerusalem peacefully for several years. Why the attack at this time?

The explanation is simple. Satan saw God's relief approaching and sought to crush the spirits of the Judean saints before it arrived. He could not stop the blessing, but he could do his diabolical worst to spoil it.

We see this same principle in David's Ziklag experience.

For many years, David waited patiently for God to deliver him from Saul. Only then could he ascend to the throne as prophesied. David realized that Saul's judgment meant personal deliverance for him and his men and the start of great blessing for all Israel. When the long-awaited day of liberation finally came, Satan tried to crush David with discouragement. Just as God was executing Saul's sentence upon Mount Gilboa, the Ziklag drama unfolded (1 Samuel 30-31). *While God was using the Philistines to judge Saul, Satan was using the Amalekites to vex David.*

The attack at Ziklag was so strong, so personal, so surprising, that David almost went under. But He encouraged himself in the Lord his God and held on. Then he pursued the Amalekites and recovered all they had stolen from him and his men. And on the third day after he returned to Ziklag, word came of Saul's death (2 Samuel 1:1-4). Like a flash of lightening, David realized what had really happened to him at Ziklag. His great distress and Saul's death had occurred *simultaneously*. Ziklag was no mere coincidence. Though *by* men, it was not *of* men. The Amalekites performed the raid, but Satan planned and inspired it. Ziklag was his well-timed blow, intended to crush David precisely when God was ready to relieve him from the rigors of his distressing wilderness trials. *Satan vexed David to the breaking point just as God's relief was finally at hand.* But David laid hold of God and did not break. He later wrote, "Thou hast thrust hard at me that I might fall, but the Lord helped me" (Psalms 118:13).

Our adversary, the devil, still works against us in this way. He often vexes us strongly, just as God's relief is fast approaching.

Why does he do this? To rob us and our God. Jesus taught, "The thief cometh not but to steal" (John 10:10). If we continue to believe and obey, Satan cannot altogether stop answers to our prayers or other blessings from getting through. But He can and will seek to vex us. He hopes to trouble us to the point that we will neither appreciate nor enjoy God's blessings, nor give God due praise, thanks, and worship as we should. Thus he seeks to steal our enjoyment and deprive God of praise. This is one of his devices: "For we are not ignorant of his devices" (2 Corinthians 2:11).

God has given us several effective countermeasures to defeat the enemy's plan.

First, by merely believing this principle we are greatly helped. When we realize that the Scriptures teach that satanic vexation is often the harbinger of divine blessing, we're immediately relieved. That is, if we choose to believe it. And we're put at a distinct advantage—for to discover the enemy's tactic is to win half the battle. From then on, every sudden onslaught of demonic resistance becomes to us a joyful announcement of imminent relief from on high. The more we meditate on this, the more we believe; and the more we believe, the more we go free from the power of vexation. Believing God's truth imparts immediate internal liberation: "The truth shall make you free . . . free indeed" (John 8:32, 36). It holds us still when everything around us suddenly goes crazy. It cools us in the heat of trial, strengthens us in the depths of weakness, and refills us when drained to the danger point: "Consider what I say, and the Lord give thee understanding in all things" (2 Timothy 2:7). The moment we consider this truth believingly, faith imparts rest and relief to our weary souls: "For we who have believed do enter into rest" (Hebrews 4:3).

Second, we must give thanks. Not *for* the vexation, but *in* it: "In every thing give thanks; for this is the will of God in Christ Jesus concerning you" (1 Thessalonians 5:18). If we believe that satanic vexation often announces coming relief, we should deliberately thank the Lord for His help. This exercises faith, for we are thanking Him before seeing His help arrive. It also glorifies God, for He is honored when we give the sacrifice of praise while trouble still swirls around us. And it helps us, for thanking and praising God soothes the chafed spirit of the praiser. The more we thank Him, the better we feel. The one that gives praise is given peace: "Give, and it shall be given unto you" (Luke 6:38).

Third, we should pray more. Increased prayer heals the vexed spirit: "Men ought always to pray, and not to faint" (Luke 18:1-8).

The Jerusalem saints overcame Herod's vicious attack by increasing their praying. The entire time Peter was in prison, they prayed continuously: "Peter, therefore, was kept in prison; but prayer was made without ceasing by the church unto God for him" (Acts 12:5). They overcame the vexer by obeying the apostolic injunction, "Pray without ceasing" (1 Thessalonians 5:17).

Through James, the Holy Spirit prescribes increased prayer as a cure for the afflicted heart: "Is any among you afflicted? Let him pray" (James 5:13).

Jesus taught that increased prayer would help make us strong, alert, and worthy in these perilous days before His appearing. When international unrest, national distress, ecclesiastical impotency, and personal stress rise to unprecedented levels, Jesus says, "Watch ye, therefore, and pray always, that ye may be accounted worthy to escape all these things that shall come to pass, and to stand before the Son of man" (Luke 21:36).

The Psalmist also turned to increased prayer when tribulation or persecution suddenly poured in: "But I give myself unto prayer" (Psalms 109:4). When Satan cast burdens on David, David cast them over on God. How? By praying "evening, and morning, and at noon" (Psalms 55:17). He counsels us to do the same: "Cast thy burden upon the Lord, and he shall sustain thee; he shall never suffer the righteous to be moved" (55:22).

Why is prayer so beneficial to tried saints? Because of the reviving effects of God's presence: "In thy presence is fullness of joy" (Psalms 16:11). The presence is more important than the petition. We should, of course, petition God for every need (Philippians 4:6-7). But soaking is more important than asking. The Lord wants us to petition Him, not only to get answers, but to spend quality time with Him. Asking gets us into the habit of abiding in His presence. Once there, God saturates us afresh with His Spirit. The longer we soak in our heavenly Father's presence, the stronger we get. His supernatural presence supernaturally restores our souls: "He restoreth my soul" (Psalms 23:3). Spirit permeates spirit, Mind meets mind, and Soul breathes life into soul. The Creator's powerful presence recreates the core of His creature. After time in His presence, we emerge thoroughly refreshed and ready to finish the race set before us.

When the enemy comes in like a flood, let us neither faint nor rebel. Let us neither cease doing God's will nor charge Him with folly. Rather, let us remember that *relief is on the way*. In one form or another, God's help is soon to arrive. It may be a manifest answer to one of our petitions, long awaited and sorely needed—a great blessing totally unexpected by us, exceedingly abundantly above anything we ever dreamed—financial aid, arriving when we could have gone no further without it— the removal of an oppressor, when further oppression would have been unbearable—full physical recovery, when prolonged illness had taxed faith and patience to the limit—or any other timely blessing that lifts the burden from our shoulders.

If we remember this and practice the countermeasures God has given us, no furious Herods or swarming Amalekites will overwhelm us. We'll stand firm until God's relief arrives.

15

"Sans Blessings" Saints

Then Satan answered the Lord, and said,
Doth Job fear God for nothing?

(Job 1:9)

"Sans" is a French word meaning "without, lacking, or in the absence of." The Scripture tells us of souls who persevered in close fellowship and faithful service to God "sans blessings,"—that is, in the absence of God's manifest blessings. During long periods of affliction and reproach, they had nothing whatsoever to show for their godliness. Believers who serve the Blesser for His blessings are common. Sans blessings saints are rare.

Job is God's greatest sans blessings saint.

Satan's insulting accusation, "Doth Job fear God for nothing?" (Job 1:9), became God's primary objective in testing Job. In short, He hoped that Job would prove Satan wrong. He set about to reduce Job, to cut him back materially, to strip away his exterior blessings until there was left, as Satan said, "nothing." Only Job's spiritual life itself was to be left untouched: "He is in thine hand; but save his life" (2:6). Why? To see if he would be as loyal and devoted without blessings as he had been with them. Job was an outstanding man during the days of his prosperity. While protected by God's hedge, he thrived spiritually and materially. Spiritually, there was "none like him in the earth" (1:8). Materially, Job was "the greatest of all the men of the east" (1:3). Surrounded with God's blessings, he was the living embodiment of godly humanity, mature in faith, love, wisdom, and the fear of the Lord: "That man was perfect and upright, and one that feared God, and shunned evil" (1:1).

But the issue at hand was this: *Would Job be the same man when stripped of all his possessions, relationships, respect, and even his health?* Would he continue to thrive spiritually? Would his love for God be undiminished and his service unchanged? This was what God sought to find out. Satan wagered that unjustified adversity would end Job's walk with God. God believed that it would not.

Satan pointed to Job's abundant blessings to prove his accusation: "Thou hast blessed the work of his hands, and his substance is increased in the land" (1:10). He claimed that if Job's manifold blessings were removed, his spiritual life would collapse, that if his prosperity were broken off, he would break off relations with God: "But put forth thine hand now, and touch all that he hath, and he will curse thee to thy face" (1:11). It was a serious charge demanding a prompt response. Therefore, the Lord accepted the challenge. Placing clear limitations on Satan's actions, He authorized the great contest: "And the Lord said unto Satan, Behold, all that he hath is in thy power; only upon himself put not forth thine hand" (1:12a). Having obtained divine permission, Satan immediately began His assault: "So Satan went forth from the presence of the Lord" (1:12b). The test was on.

For nine to twelve months, Job suffered intensely (Job 1:13 - 42:9). Every token of divine approval was stripped away. Children, possessions, health, friends, respect, everything was taken from him. His entire being was shot through with pain—mental, emotional, and physical. In agony, he cried out to God. He contended with his critics, he questioned, he complained. But never did he renounce his faith. Through it all, he trusted that God had the answers he did not have. Thus, the end Satan hoped for never materialized. Though severely shaken, the man Job stood true to God. The father of lies was thus proven a liar and God was vindicated.

Job's lengthy ordeal established the fact that he would serve God for nothing. When temporarily stripped of all that he had, and that without cause, he still maintained his walk with God. God said to Satan, "And still he holdeth fast his integrity, although thou movedst me against him, to destroy him without cause" (2:3).

But Job's trial proved more than his personal integrity. Satan's insult implied that all of God's servants serve Him only for what they get from Him, for temporal material benefits. Job's loyal endurance, sans blessings, proves forever that, although the undevoted majority serve God for His blessings, there exists a devoted minority who will cleave unto Him and do His will, even for nothing. These true servants, God's overcomers, serve Him for Himself: "And His servants shall serve Him" (Revelation 22:3). Irrespective of identifiable blessings or lack of them, they "cling unto the Lord" with "purpose of heart" (Acts 11:23). Neither poverty nor prosperity move them from Him. Their contentment lies solely in knowing that they are pleasing the heavenly Father: "I do always those things that please him" (John 8:29). Their abiding joy lies not in external things, but in their private fellowship with their Lord. Their sense of purpose is focused on faithfully executing their duties in their current field of service, large or small. Knowing that it is His will makes their task satisfying: "My food is to do the will of him that sent me, and to finish his work" (John 4:34). Although some men count them useless, they are extremely useful to God. Such are the characteristics of souls like Job.

Lesser servants—Demas types—come and go with God's material blessings. When blessings abound, they abound. Wherever success and prosperity appear, they appear. While prosperous, they are happy and reasonably dedicated. But as soon as adverse conditions arise, they waver. Their dedication slackens, then ceases. They forsake their God-given duties and faithful brethren: "For Demas hath forsaken me, having loved this present world" (2 Timothy 4:10). They wander off to their own life, their own way, and their own goals. Spiritually, they curse God and die, and return to their former idols. These serve God, not for Himself, but for His blessing. So when it departs, they depart.

The Scriptures tell us of other sans blessings saints. Elijah was reduced to bread, flesh, and water by the brook for a season. But he remained content and in such close fellowship with God that he detected His voice the instant He spoke, ordering him to Zarephath (1 Kings 17:2-7). Joseph had his earthly father's favor stripped away while he was a slave and a prisoner in Egypt. But he continued to serve his heavenly Father faithfully, first in Potiphar's house, then in the prison (Genesis 37; 39-40). Moses, blessed with the comfort and wealth of Egypt, was drastically reduced when constrained to live the lifestyle of a desert shepherd for forty years. But in that humble setting, he kept the vision and "endured, as seeing him who is invisible" (Hebrews 11:27). Christian fellowship was stripped away from the apostle John when he was exiled on the Isle of Patmos, yet he remained in fellowship with Christ. He was "in the Spirit on the Lord's day" in the midst of his isolation (Revelation 1:9-10). These continued to love and serve God when they were abased (Philippians 4:11-12). They were content in Him even when cut back to life's barest essentials: "And having food and raiment let us be therewith content" (1 Timothy 6:8). Sans blessings, their spiritual life continued to thrive.

God tested Job severely, but not forever. There came an end: "And the Lord turned the captivity of Job, when he prayed for his friends" (Job 42:10). When Job reached the other side of his trial, to his utter amazement, he found even greater blessings than those he had had before being tested: "The Lord gave Job twice as much as he had before . . . So the Lord blessed the latter end of Job more than his beginning" (Job 42:10, 12).

In Job's experience, this truth is evident: *God saves His greatest blessings for those who serve Him without blessings.* Those who walk closely with God with no portion can be trusted with His "double portion" (Isaiah 61:7). When we serve Him faithfully with an empty fold, He can safely grant us His "hundredfold" (Mark 10:30).

The only Bible character specifically said to have received a hundredfold earthly blessing is Isaac: "Then Isaac sowed in that land, and received in the same year an hundredfold: and the Lord blessed him. And the man waxed great, and went forward, and grew until he became very great; for he had possession of flocks, and possession of herds, and great store of servants" (Genesis 26:12-14). Yet it should be noted that before Isaac received this tremendous blessing from God, he first proved his willingness to serve God without blessings, even unto death. On Mount Moriah, Isaac offered neither objection nor resistance to Abraham as he moved to put him to death (Genesis 22:1-10). In ultimate submission and trust, he laid down his very life to do the will of his God and his father. His amazing submission foreshadows the coming sacrifice of the Son of God. Therefore, Isaac had laid down everything—his manifest blessings and life itself—before he received the hundredfold blessing of God.

To the rich young ruler, Jesus made no promises of earthly blessing. He promised only that if he would sell out, he would qualify for treasure in heaven: "Sell whatever thou hast, and give to the poor, and thou shalt have treasure in heaven; and come, take up the cross, and follow me" (Mark 10:21). But this young man thought more of his blessings than of the Blesser. Unwilling to lay down either his blessings or his life, He "went away grieved" (10:22).

But to the apostles, Jesus promised "an hundredfold now in this time, houses, and brethren, and sisters, and mothers, and children, and lands, with persecutions, and in the age to come eternal life" (10:29-30). Why? Because they had left all to follow the Master: "Lo, we have left all, and have followed thee" (10:28). Homes, lands, wives, children, careers, relations—at God's call, the apostles laid aside all these blessed things: "And when they had brought their boats to land, they forsook all and followed him" (Luke 5:11). They paid the price the rich young ruler was unwilling to pay. He rejected the cross. They received and carried it. He held fast his possessions. They let go of theirs. He would not serve God sans blessings. They did. Hence, they qualified for God's greatest blessings. He did not.

Beloved, the God who tested Job must test us. For our adversary, the devil, who spoke against Job, has also reproached us. Of this generation of Christians he has said, "Do they serve God for nothing?" To answer this serious charge, God must test us. In the coming days, all believers will pass through a degree of testing similar to Job's. The details of our trials—the severity, duration, costs, and rewards—will vary, but all will be put to the test. God must find out where each of us stands, whom we really serve, what we really seek.

God knows that we will sing His praises while we are prosperous, popular, and successful. *But will we be the same worshipers when we are cut back, reduced, and stripped of all evidence of divine approval?* What if God should permit Satan to break through our hedge and steal possessions, relationships, reputation, and even health from us for a season? Will we still cleave to God and be in the Spirit on the Lord's day? Will persecution mean the end of our fellowship with God or the beginning of a new depth of sainthood? Will we draw back or go on unto perfection? Will we curse God and die or trust Him and grow? Will we prove Satan right or stop the mouth of the adversary?

God is earnestly seeking answers to these questions. At this moment, He is searching through His worldwide congregation for sans blessings saints. Are you willing to pay the price to be among them? Will you serve God for *nothing*?

16

Where to Turn When Others Turn Away

> *To him that is afflicted, pity should be shown from his friend, but . . . my brethren [friends] have dealt deceitfully . . .*

(Job 6:14-15)

In Job's severe hour of trial, his closest friends took a surprising turn. Just when he expected them to understand and be supportive, they judged and criticized him instead. It was the third major blow that Satan dealt the man Job. The first two failed to shake him. This one hit its mark.

Amazingly, Job overcame the bitter loss of his children and property (Job 1:13-22).

He further endured the loss of his health with a steadfast spirit (Job 2:1-10).

But when his closest friends turned against him, that was it. At that point, Job lost his remarkable composure. He did not renounce his faith in God, as Satan had hoped, but he did complain against

God profusely and argue with his friends heatedly from then on. Not until God's eventual rebuke did Job regain his spiritual attitude.

Job was comforted at first by the mere presence of his friends: "Now when Job's three friends heard of all this evil that was come upon him, they came . . . to mourn with him and to comfort him" (Job 2:11). He had lost everything but them. When they arrived, his heart must have breathed fresh hope. Now maybe things would begin to get better. He desperately anticipated their sympathetic support. After all, "a friend loveth at all times, and a brother is born for adversity" (Proverbs 17:17). At first they gave him what he hoped for: "They sat down with him upon the ground . . . and none spoke a word unto him; for they saw that his grief was very great" (2:12-13). Their silent support, however, lasted only a week—"seven days and seven nights" (2:13).

As soon as Job began to cry out in anguish, however, his former supporters turned on him and quickly became his worst enemies. When they launched into their merciless criticism of him, Job was bitterly disappointed. He had looked for refreshment as from the brook of friendship, but to no avail (Job 6:14-21). His brook was dried up. In the throes of tribulation, Job was left completely without human support.

There was no help for him then except in God.

Job, however, could find no comfort in God. He was huffed and irritated with the Almighty over the turn his friends had taken. When others turned away, he blamed God for their treatment of him and refused to look up for inspiration. Offended with his Lord, Job cut himself off from his only remaining source of help: "When affliction or trouble or persecution comes on account of the Word, at once he is caused to stumble—he is repelled and begins to distrust and desert Him Whom he ought to trust and obey, and he falls away" (Matthew 13:21, AMP). His superior spirituality then quickly began to unravel. Had it not been for God's merciful correction, Job may have remained defeated permanently.

By contrast, David learned where to turn when others turn away.

Before Saul forced him to flee for his life, David was loved and respected by all Israel. He was widely known as a man of deep faith, a dedicated shepherd, a courageous warrior, a captain in the army, a skilled musician, and son-in-law to the King. The man who recommended him before Saul described him as "a son of Jesse, the Bethlehemite, who is skillful in playing, and a mighty, valiant man, and a man of war, and prudent in matters, and an agreeable person, and the Lord is with him" (1 Samuel 16:18). After David defeated Goliath and the Philistines, all Israel shared this admiration: "All Israel and Judah loved David, because he went out and came in before them . . . so that his name was much esteemed" (1 Samuel 18:16, 30). He was a youthful, living legend, a man whom thousands hoped would build a prosperous future for their nation. Every Israelite was a friend to David and he was one to them. Leaders and people alike held him in high esteem: "Then Ahimelech answered the king, and said, And who is so faithful among all thy servants as David, who is the king's son-in-law, and goeth at thy bidding, and is honorable in thine house?" (1 Samuel 22:14).

King Saul's slander campaign, however, changed all of this. Moved by envy, Saul circulated a vicious lie about David. He reported that David and his men, at Jonathan's instigation, were plotting to overthrow him: "Then Saul said unto his servants who stood about him . . . my son hath made a league with the son of Jesse . . . my son hath stirred up my servant against me, to lie in wait, as at this day" (1 Samuel 22:6-9). This, of course, was the reason the king was forced to go out and extinguish the life of his own son-in-law. Or at least, so he said.

As ridiculous as this report was, it nevertheless gained strength as time passed. The longer God waited to vindicate David, while Saul remained in power and unjudged, the worse David looked. After all, if God was with David, why didn't He help him? Why didn't He intervene? Judging only by what they could see, the people assumed that Saul had told the truth and soon forgot all that David had been and done. As the years passed away, so did David's former reputation. The entire nation gradually lost faith in the son of Jesse.

The Scriptures make this evident.

In Keilah, David and his men risked their lives to deliver the city from the Philistines (1 Samuel 23:1-13). But immediately afterwards, the men of Keilah were ready to deliver them into Saul's hands. So God warned David to flee. Why were the men of Keilah so unfaithful to David after he showed them such kindness? Apparently, they no longer believed God was with him. It was a bitter disappointment to the future king.

The men of Ziph also turned against David (1 Samuel 23:14-25). When he and his men came there, the Ziphites went straight to Saul to inform him of David's presence in their land. They agreed to deliver him over to the king and his army as soon as they could come. David again escaped. But once more, human helpers had failed him.

When David's company lacked food, he sent messengers to Nabal, a wealthy sheep herder, asking him for provisions (1 Samuel 25:1-39). David's men had protected Nabal's flocks in times past without asking for or receiving pay for their services. He hoped now that Nabal would return the favor. But not Nabal. He hastily rejected David's request. And his insulting reply makes it clear that His opinion of David had changed drastically. He, too, believed Saul's report: "Who is David? And who is the son of Jesse? There are many servants nowadays who break away, every man from his master" (25:10).

To top it all off, David's own men turned on him at Ziklag (1 Samuel 30:1-6). Deeply grieved at the apparent loss of their wives and children, David's men "lifted up their voice and wept, until they had no more power to weep . . . because the soul of all the people was grieved, every man for his sons and for his daughters" (30:4, 6b). Their grief soon turned to anger and their anger immediately turned toward David and "the people spoke of stoning him" (30:6a). This was the lowest moment in David's long wilderness tribulation. It was his midnight hour. Great adversity lay upon him and now all his friends had turned away. He was without a single shred of human support.

This was exactly the position Job was in. But note carefully David's different reaction: "David encouraged himself in the Lord his God" (30:6c). When others turned away, David turned hard to God. He looked up toward heaven with everything in him: "I looked on my right hand, and beheld, but there was no man that would know me. Refuge failed me; no man cared for my soul. I cried unto thee, O Lord. I said, Thou art my refuge" (Psalms 142:4-5).

By making some quality choices, David escaped the pit of offense into which Job fell.

First, he chose to not be offended with God at his severe test: "Great peace have they who love thy law, and nothing shall offend them" (Psalms 119:165)—"And blessed is he, whosoever shall not be offended in me" (Luke 7:23).

Second, he chose not to fret himself at the evildoers who refused to help him: "Fret not thyself because of evildoers . . . fret not thyself because of him who prospereth in his way, because of the man who bringeth wicked devices to pass" (Psalms 37:1, 7). Rather than self-destruct through anger, David chose to trust in, delight in, and commit his worries to God, with decisiveness, finality, and thanksgiving: "Trust in the Lord . . . delight thyself also in the Lord . . . Commit thy way unto the Lord . . . and he shall bring it to pass" (37:3-5).

Third, he chose to forgive his close friends who turned against him in his hour of distress: "Forgive, if ye have anything against any, that your Father also, who is in heaven, may forgive you your trespasses. But if ye do not forgive, neither will your Father, who is in heaven, forgive your trespasses" (Mark 11:25-26)—"And forgive us our debts, as we forgive our debtors" (Matthew 6:12).

Fourth, he chose to look away from it all to his unfailing heavenly friend: "There is a friend who sticketh closer than a brother" (Proverbs 18:24). When human support failed, divine support prevailed. When his brothers' grace was insufficient, David found the Lord's grace more than sufficient: "My grace is sufficient for thee" (2 Corinthians 12:9). Even at Ziklag, David found all the comfort his soul needed. So much that, with God's help, he rose up and pursued his enemies and recovered all that had been stolen from him (1 Samuel 30:18-19).

Let us study and learn from Job's error and David's triumph. Henceforth, when human comforters fail us, let us seek our consolation in God. When others turn away, let us turn hard to the One who never turns away, our ever-faithful friend, Jesus.

> For he hath said, I will never leave thee, nor forsake thee.
>
> So that we may boldly say, The Lord is my helper, and I will not fear what man shall do unto me.
>
> (Hebrews 13:5-6)

17

Trouble in the Center of His Will

> . . . *tribulation or persecution ariseth because of the Word . . .*
>
> (Matthew 13:21)

When we meet trouble, we often think that it must have arisen because we disobeyed our Lord. Sometime, somewhere, somehow we displeased Him.

For instance, Jonah's rebellion landed him in a fish's belly, Jacob's procrastination led to tragedy at Shechem, and Lot's selfish choice cost him everything when Sodom was finally destroyed. So, if we meet with roadblocks, perplexities, and persistent opposition, disobedience must be the cause of our trouble. Right? No, not necessarily.

You see, *God's perfect will always includes a measure of trouble.* Adversity is His age-old instrument with which He tests His children and builds up our characters. The Scriptures make this clear. Consider the following examples.

God expressly led Isaac to sojourn in Gerar: "And the Lord appeared unto him, and said, Go not down into Egypt; dwell in the land which I shall tell thee of. Sojourn in this land" (Genesis 26:2-3). Isaac submitted and obeyed: "And Isaac dwelt in Gerar" (26:6). Yet soon afterwards, he ran into trouble. Stirred by envy, the Philistines ran him out of town: "And Abimelech said unto Isaac, Go from us" (26:16). Later they strove with him over the wells his servants had dug, wells that belonged to his father before him (26:15, 17-25). Isaac, a peaceful man, found that obedience sometimes causes strife and division to arise.

As Joseph sought only to obey and please his father's God, he found himself sold as a slave by his own brothers (Genesis 37:1-36). As he went further in God's chosen way, he was falsely accused, convicted, and imprisoned—all because he would *not* disobey and "sin against God" (39:9). Strangely, the more Joseph obeyed, the deeper he got into trouble. Stranger still, the more Joseph plunged into adversity, the closer God drew near: "But the Lord was with Joseph, and showed him mercy, and gave him favor in the sight of the keeper of the prison" (39:21).

The Lord led Moses to return to Egypt to deliver the children of Israel. But at first, Moses' return caused the peoples' sufferings to increase, not decrease: "And Moses returned unto the Lord, and said, 'Lord, wherefore hast thou so badly treated this people? Why is it that thou hast sent me? For since I came to Pharaoh to speak in thy name, he hath done evil to this people; neither hast thou delivered thy people at all'" (Exodus 5:22-23).

Later, the Spirit of God explicitly ordered Moses to lead the Israelites to the scene of their harrowing Red Sea experience: "And the Lord spoke unto Moses, saying, Speak unto the children of Israel, that they turn and encamp before Pi-hahiroth, between Migdol and the sea, over against Baal-zephon; before it shall ye encamp by the sea" (Exodus 14:1-2). Although they obeyed, it looked like certain death there until the Almighty intervened.

Afterwards, the Lord led the Israelites into a trouble-filled time of testing in the wilderness. There, in the center of His will, they faced a wide array of difficulties and hardships: "Who led thee through that great and terrible wilderness, wherein were fiery serpents, and scorpions, and drought, where there was no water" (Deuteronomy 8:15-16).

Finally, when it was God's time for Joshua to lead Israel across the Jordan to take possession of the promised land, the ultimate trouble—war—lay in the center of the divinely-marked pathway. God was commanding, Joshua was leading, and Israel was obeying, but still war had to be faced.

The Holy Spirit led Jesus straight into a head-on confrontation with the devil himself: "And Jesus, being full of the Holy Spirit, returned from the Jordan, and was led by the Spirit into the wilderness, being forty days tested by the devil" (Luke 4:1-2). Before the heavenly Father would commission His Son for ministry, Jesus had to meet and overcome the ultimate troubler. Our Captain's personal testing had to be finished and complete: "For it became him . . . to make the captain of their salvation perfect through sufferings" (Hebrews 2:10).

The Holy Spirit told Peter and the apostles to "Go, stand and speak in the temple to the people all the words of this life" (Acts 5:20). They promptly obeyed. But what followed their obedience? A successful meeting with positive results? No, they were immediately arrested for the second time and narrowly escaped execution.

The Spirit of God forbade Paul and Silas to minister in either Asia or Bithynia and strongly urged them instead to go into Macedonia (Acts 16:6-10). What did their obedience bring? Did all Macedonia turn to the Lord? No, Paul found favor with one upright woman and her family and a single church was established. Not long afterwards, he was beaten publicly and jailed without a trial (16:16-40). But he was in the center of God's will nonetheless.

Years later in Jerusalem, the Lord appeared to Paul and told him plainly that he must go to Rome in the days ahead: "And the night following the Lord stood by him, and said, Be of good cheer, Paul; for as thou hast testified of me in Jerusalem, so must thou bear witness also at Rome" (Acts 23:11). Yet how strange and turbulent was Paul's divinely-plotted course. He encountered unjust court hearings, death plots, a lengthy prison stay, and a near disastrous voyage at sea in which he experienced a fierce hurricane, a violent shipwreck, and a deadly snake bite (Acts 24-26; 23:12-21; 24:24-27; 27:1-44; 28:1-6).

Often Paul found *nothing but trouble* in the center of God's will!

In each of the above examples, we see that God's servants frequently ran into trouble, not because they disobeyed, but because they obeyed. All these problems befell them in the center of God's perfect plan. So, obviously, the presence of trouble is no proof that we have disobeyed God or missed His leading. Rather, it is often divine confirmation— God's subtle way of reassuring the spiritually minded that they are indeed doing His will.

The enemy doesn't bother with us when we're deceived, distracted, or disobedient. He likes us that way and is quite content to let us be. But as soon as we turn to obey God, we immediately pose a threat to Satan's kingdom. If we persist, if we press on, we'll bear fruit unto God. We'll become strong and stable and through us others will be enlightened, delivered, and comforted. Most importantly, God will be glorified through our lives. This the enemy cannot chance. He therefore comes after us with all the irritation and vexation he can muster. His strategy is simply to make life miserable for all obedient saints, hoping thereby to dissuade us from continuing to do our Lord's will: "There was given to me a thorn in the flesh, the messenger of Satan to buffet me" (2 Corinthians 12:7). This is what Jesus had in mind when He taught us that "tribulation or persecution ariseth because of the Word" (Matthew 13:21).

In case any of us, unusually pressed of late by our adversary, are tempted to turn aside from obedience to escape this pressure, let us remember this: *Disobedience will cost us far more later on than obedience will cost us now.* Both the obedient and the disobedient Christian pay a price. The obedient one pays up front; he obeys and takes the consequences now, trusting the Lord to deliver, reward, and honor him in His time. The children of disobedience compromise their way out of trouble for the present, only to pay a much higher price later on—and without any reward.

Initially, Abraham paid a high cost to obey the call of God—separation, hardship, uncertainty, and unrealized hopes during a long period of waiting. But in his latter days he experienced great fruitfulness, blessing, joy, and honor: "And so, after he had patiently endured, he obtained the promise" (Hebrews 6:15). Abraham received the "end of the Lord" because he obeyed all the way through (James 5:11). His guiding principle was to obey God whatever the cost. Although he was rarely trouble-free, he kept himself in God's will, the place of blessing.

Lot, however, avoided all trouble and hardship by choosing for self, not God's will, in every conflict. Apparently his guiding principle was, "My will be done, whether it's Thine or not." And for years he appeared to have made it. He was a respected, prosperous man in Sodom, holding an undisclosed position of authority. But in one swift stroke of judgment, his false prosperity was stripped away. God's collection agents finally overtook him. When they finished their work, Lot had nothing. Everything he had striven to save, he lost—position, possessions, reputation, wife, sons-in-law, and his testimony. And these belated sufferings earned him no rewards. Although saved as by fire, Lot's life ended a total loss: "If any man's work shall be burned, he shall suffer loss; but he himself shall be saved, yet as by fire" (1 Corinthians 3:15).

Our Master summed up this spiritual law when He said, "He that findeth his life shall lose it; and he that loseth his life for my sake shall find it" (Matthew 10:39). Brethren, be wise. Be willing to do anything—lose, suffer, forego, pay, wait, be mocked—but stay in the will of God! Remember that trouble will come even there, and determine not to allow the enemy's pressure to drive you out of your place of blessing.

18

Victory the Hard Way

And there came against Gibeah 10,000 chosen men out of all Israel, and the battle was hard...

(Judges 20:34, AMP)

Israel's brief civil war teaches us an unusual pathway to victory (Judges 20:1-48).

In most of Israel's conflicts, she routed her enemies as soon as the battle was joined. As long as the people were pursuing God's will, the Lord smote, slew, and prevailed over the opposition. In short order the chosen nation was delivered and her enemies vanquished. This was the norm for Israel in the day of battle.

But in Israel's conflict with the tribe of Benjamin, victory came a different way. This conflict was neither quick nor easy. It was hard fought, costly, and slow in coming. God let the righteous suffer. He permitted them to fall before strengthening them to stand. They experienced sorrow before joy. They tasted two stunning defeats before savoring victory on the "third day" (Judges 20:30). This is victory the hard way—victory through the midst of defeat.

It appears at first that God let Israel suffer as punishment for the prevailing apostasy among them. And truly they were far from perfect. In the days of the judges, "every man did that which was right in his own eyes" (Judges 21:25). Sin, unbelief, and idolatry abounded. Righteous living was the exception and not the rule.

Yet the Israelites' substandard spiritual condition was not the reason for their two defeats at the hand of the Benjamites. They were far more righteous than their depraved brethren who defended sodomites and rapists (Judges 19 & 20). God did not have to take counsel to decide which of the two warring factions He should support. The issue was not clouded. God's sentiments were strong and His will clear. He was behind the united tribes of Israel one hundred percent in their effort to purge the moral cancer growing in Benjamin that threatened the very life of their nation.

Nevertheless, the Israelites were severely defeated in the first two battles. Thousands of their men died. The situation was baffling, a complete mystery to faith. The sinful had defeated the righteous. The ungodly had smitten the godly. Morality had fallen before immorality. God appeared to favor the Benjamites. The Israelites were entirely in God's will, in complete unity, in faith, and under the Lord's direct leading. Yet they were still defeated, not once but *twice*. Why? Because God was teaching them, educating them, training them in His hard way.

This is how Israel's severe test unfolded.

A grievous sin arose among them. Sodomy had been revived among the saints. The men of Gibeah were living exactly like the men of Sodom (Judges 19:1-28). Their sin reached the breaking point when they raped and killed the concubine of a visiting Levite. The other eleven tribes reacted decisively. They would not tolerate the sin of Gibeah another day. It had to go. First they offered to execute only the men that assaulted the Levite's concubine: "Now, therefore, deliver to us the men, the base fellows, who are in Gibeah" (Judges 20:13a). But this reasonable offer was rejected by the backslidden Benjamites: "But the children of Benjamin would not hearken to the voice of their brethren, the children of Israel" (20:13b). The only alternative left was war.

So the eleven tribes gathered at Mizpah to seek God's direction and help in the stern duty that lay before them. Their cause was just. They sought not to conquer and spoil the innocent. Rather, they sought to exterminate sin before it brought extinctive judgment on the chosen people. They warred only to protect their peace and liberty. They killed only to preserve life.

But, "the battle was hard" (Judges 20:34, AMP). For two consecutive days, the Israelites attacked. Each day they experienced fierce combat, suffered casualties, regrouped, and asked counsel of the Lord again. Then, after two costly defeats, they had to gather up their faith and courage and attack one more time. As never before, this generation of Israelites had to *persevere*.

They had to exercise their faith to the limit. They had to ignore the two fresh defeats they had seen:

"While we look not at the things which are seen, but at the things which are not seen; for the things which are seen are temporal, but the things which are not seen are eternal" (2 Corinthians 4:18). They had to brush aside their own baffled sense of justice and flatly refuse to be overwhelmed by discouragement. There was simply no explanation for what God had allowed to happen.

God had ordered their attack, they did not go at their own initiative. They were doing God's will, not their own. They were unified, not divided. They were in faith, not doubt. They were sanctified and without secret sins in their midst. All things considered, they should have had a mighty victory when the first swords clashed. Instead, they met defeat—costly, bitter defeat, and that for two days running. What a strange trial this was. In going to battle the third day, the Israelites had to ignore the pain of their previous experiences and step out in faith on the naked Word of God.

It should be noted that until this point, God did not promise them the time of victory. In His two previous instructions to the Israelites, the Lord told them only to "Go," giving no specific promise of an immediate victory. But now, on the eve of the third day, when Phinehas asked Him about fighting again, He reveals the specific time when victory will be seen: "Shall I yet again go out to battle against the children of Benjamin, my brother, or shall I cease? And the Lord said, Go up; for tomorrow I will deliver them into thine hand" (20:28). This time, things would be different. Despite the two previous setbacks, they would go to battle and win. And win they did: "And the Lord smote Benjamin before Israel" (20:35). The circumstances were the same, but the outcome was totally different.

Our Lord Jesus also walked in this hard way in the days of His flesh. God could have taken Him straight to heavenly glory without any suffering. But He did not. He allowed Jesus to suffer. The powers of darkness prevailed over Him in the grave for two consecutive days. Like the hard-pressed Israelites, victory came for the Son of God on "the third day" (Matthew 16:21). Through the humiliation of the Cross, Jesus obtained the honor of the resurrection. He tasted defeat before He savored victory. God let Him fall before He stood. The Captain of our salvation learned obedience, not by easy victories, but "by the things which he suffered" (Hebrews 5:8). Therefore, the hard way is Jesus' way.

God could give us quick, easy victories in every trial if He so desired. But He does not. At times He allows us to partake of His hard way. Why? Because He wants to conform us to the image of His Son: "For whom he did foreknow, he also did predestinate to be conformed to the image of his Son, that he might be the firstborn among many brethren" (Romans 8:29). He's preparing us to live eternally with Jesus and the saints. How can we truly fellowship with the crucified Christ if we've never known defeat? How would no-cost Christians feel if they were seated beside martyred prophets at the great marriage supper or permitted to live in New Jerusalem beside Christians who were faithful unto death? So God lets us suffer to make us like the King and his subjects: "All your persecutions and tribulations that ye endure . . . that ye may be counted worthy of the kingdom of God, for which ye also suffer" (2 Thessalonians 1:4-5).

The twentieth chapter of the Book of Judges proves this: *Even in doing God's will we may suffer stunning temporary defeats.* When this happens, we must not misunderstand God's dealings with us. We must not succumb to anger, reasoning, or unbelief. Rather, we must do what the Israelites did after their painful defeats. We must regroup, not retreat. We must inquire again of the Lord, not cease praying. And after we are reassured of His will, we must go up to our battle again and face the scene of our previous defeats without fear of failure. Although we have suffered setbacks, our God is still with us. We would rather win our conflicts outright from the first. But, if need be, we will obtain our victories through the midst of defeats. We have only to *persevere* and God will soon show Himself to be for us and against our Benjamites: "Though I walk in the midst of trouble, thou wilt revive me; thou shalt stretch forth thine hand against the wrath of mine enemies, and thy right hand shall save me" (Psalms 138:7).

In this instant age we've become spoiled. Everything we want we obtain quickly. We've virtually eliminated the waiting process from many common daily tasks. When we come to God, most of us bring with us a deep-seated haste, a demand for instant gratification in the things of God. We want our prayers answered, and now! But the eternal God is unhasting and unchanging. He does not cater to human impatience. If we are to know Him, love Him, walk with Him, and receive from Him, we must learn to wait. If we believe and obey, God will always give us victory as promised. But not always when we want it. Satisfaction may not come until the third day.

The hard way is the only way to full spiritual maturity. It's the way of Christ, the way of the Cross and the resurrection. Will you be one of the few who submit to it?

> Hard is the way, which leadeth unto life, and few there be that find it.
>
> (Matthew 7:14)

19

The Price of Fruitfulness

Yea, and all that will live godly in Christ Jesus shall suffer persecution.

(2 Timothy 3:12)

Fruitful servants of God often find themselves beset before and behind by the troubling of the devil. But this is the unavoidable price of fruitfulness.

Jesus' visit to Gerasa illustrates this for us (Luke 8:22-37). The Lord left the relatively peaceful city of Capernaum to go on a mission for His Father. A strongly bound demoniac was to be liberated. To do this, however, Jesus had to endure trouble both before and after His work of deliverance. First, He passed through a terrific storm while crossing the Sea of Galilee. It was a storm so perilous that even though some of His disciples were experienced seamen, they panicked for fear (8:24).

Then after the man of Gerasa was set free, Jesus experienced a very rude reception by the residents of that area: "Then the whole multitude of the country of the Gerasenes round about, besought him to depart from them" (8:37). But Jesus took it all in stride. Why? He knew that trouble was the price of fruitfulness, and accomplishing His Father's will meant more to Him than a trouble-free existence.

Jesus always considered things from a spiritual viewpoint. He looked beyond natural considerations, and estimated people and events by the spiritual factors involved.

He recognized the ferocious storm on the Sea of Galilee as Satan's desperate onslaught against Him and His little band of deliverers. It was a collective effort of the powers of the air to try to stop the deliverance of one of their most prized captives, the 'wild man' of Gerasa. To Jesus, such supernatural opposition was to be expected. It was part of His job.

After turning the demons out of the man, Jesus did not let His guard down. He knew better. Fruit had been borne, the Father was well pleased, and Satan would be furious about it all. Hence, the Lord saw His surprising rejection by the Gerasenes spiritually. He was not wrestling with flesh and blood. It was the devil expressing his displeasure at Jesus through the locals. *Just as the storming Sea of Galilee was Satan's veiled attempt to get to Jesus before the mighty deliverance could occur, so the Gerasenes' rejection was his attempt to offend Him after His work was done.* As was often the case, Jesus found Himself beset before and behind with trouble as He steadily pressed ahead bearing fruit.

Not surprisingly, He taught us this very thing. In the fifteenth chapter of John's Gospel, the Lord discussed abiding (15:1-7; 9-15), fruitfulness (15:8; 16-17), and persecution (15:18-21). In this passage, there is a natural progression of thought, an intentional sequence to the subjects Jesus is teaching. The subjects change from abiding to fruitfulness to persecution. This sequence conveys a subtle underlying message: *Abiding brings forth fruit and fruit brings with it trouble.* If we abide close to the Lord and His Word, we'll be fruitful in God. In turn, this fruitfulness will cause us to be beset before and behind by the troubling of the devil just as it did Jesus. That is, of course, unless we tire of the trouble and stop abiding. Then the tribulation and persecution will cease. But so will our fruitfulness and part in the will of God (see 1 Samuel 27:1-7).

The Lord taught openly that tribulation, persecution, and affliction must arise whenever men receive, do, or minister His Word fruitfully: "... tribulation or persecution ariseth because of the word ..." (Matthew 13:21). But we don't seem to believe Him, even though this principle is seen clearly in His and Paul's ministries and in the early days of the Church. The Book of Acts is filled with miraculous fruitfulness accompanied by relentless persecution. Yet we imagine that it will be different with us. It will not. It cannot be different. The spirit of the devil is still set in fierce opposition to the Spirit of Christ. Darkness still hates the light. Truth is still scorned by iniquity. True Christianity and apostate Christendom still abide at the opposite poles of the spiritual world. False workers are just as determined to stop true disciples today as the scribes and Pharisees were to arrest our Lord and His apostles. If we're not experiencing periodic trouble from the enemy, we're not bearing fruit for God. It's as simple as that.

When we dread trouble to the point that we try to avoid it or pray it away into thin air, we err.

We're denying a fundamental decree of God. He has declared trouble to be the price of fruitfulness until Christ returns. This is, therefore, an unchangeable law of spiritual life, a universal Christian fact. And facts cannot be shooed away. They must be faced and dealt with.

This is evident on the field of battle. Soldiers can't be heroes unless they're willing to expose themselves to enemy fire. If they stay hidden away in a bunker, they can do no exploits. They'll be safe, but unfruitful. They'll never accomplish things for their commanding officers and country nor take vital ground from the enemy. To be effective and fruitful, soldiers must accept the inevitable price of exposure to enemy fire.

Many Christians are like foolish soldiers. They want a chest full of medals for doing nothing. They like to talk about spiritual warfare, the full armor of God, and the strategies of the devil, but when it comes right down to it, they choke. They flatly refuse to do anything that might in any way make trouble for them. In imagination they dream of receiving heroes' honors, while in reality they refuse to leave the safety of lukewarm Christianity. They consistently choose the path of least resistance, whether that means doing God's will or failing Him. Dedicated to no-risk living, they leave other, braver saints to stand fast against the enemy's onslaughts.

Jesus did not do this. As the "captain of the host of the Lord" (Joshua 5:14), He set an example for us in valor. As seen in Gerasa, He systematically pursued and took all His Father's objectives, knowing all along that the enemy would be after Him. Throughout the Gospel record, the 'Good

Soldier' wrought miracles and taught truth while constantly under fire from Satan's agents. Jesus' hometown rejected Him violently, the religious leaders denounced Him, His brothers mocked Him, Herod threatened Him, one of His own apostles betrayed Him, and His own nation cried out for His execution. It was a high price, but He paid it willingly to win His Father's battles. And although He was often wounded and finally killed, in the end He won—for His Father, for Himself, and for us all.

If we're trying to bear fruit unto God and avoid trouble at the same time, we're wasting all our efforts in a pitiful exercise in futility. We're trying to do something our Master could not do. And we're showing God, angels, discerning saints, and the enemy that we don't know much about spiritual warfare.

Cowards spend all their thought, time, and energy trying to avoid inevitable confrontations. Courageous souls accept the unpleasant facts of war, put on their armor, and go forth to bear fruit under fire: "The people that do know their God shall be strong, and do exploits" (Daniel 11:32). Throughout the history of human conflict, cowards have never won a war. They never will. And our God will never use them in the ongoing conflict between the true Church and the world.

May God grant us the wisdom to accept trouble as the price of fruitfulness, and the willingness and courage to endure it as good soldiers.

> Thou, therefore, endure hardness, as a good soldier of Jesus Christ.
>
> (2 Timothy 2:3)

20

We Must Be Courageous

*Arise; for this matter belongeth unto thee . . .
be of good courage, and do it.*

(Ezra 10:4)

It takes courage to obey God. And the further we go in obedience, the more courage it takes. Biblical discipleship is not for the faint of heart.

Looking around us in the Church today, it's obvious that real courage is rare. We're blessed with spiritual knowledge, material resources, and God-given opportunities, yet we're still coming short of the purpose of God. We wander in the wilderness of lukewarm Christianity when we should have occupied the promised land of spiritual maturity long ago. Why? Because we lack the moral strength to act on the knowledge God has given us. Or more specifically, we lack the courage to fully do God's Word.

Webster's defines courage as "the attitude of facing and dealing with anything recognized as

161

dangerous, difficult, or painful instead of withdrawing from it." This definition also helps us define an antonym for courage. Cowardice is simply the reverse of the above. It's "the attitude of withdrawing from anything recognized as dangerous, difficult, or painful instead of facing and dealing with it." What the courageous soul faces and deals with, the coward considers and flees from. One stands fast, while the other runs fast. One withstands, while the other withdraws: "The wicked flee when no man pursueth, but the righteous are bold as a lion" (Proverbs 28:1).

A common misconception is that courageous folks have no fears, that they simply do not feel the hesitancy, the quiverings, the shakiness the rest of us feel. But this is not true. At least, not at first. Courageous souls *do* have fears like everyone else. They just refuse to succumb to them.

Courageous Christians learn that whenever God speaks they must overrule fear and obey, acting upon their courageous instincts. Cowardly Christians hesitate and hesitate and hesitate, until their fears have smothered all their braver inclinations.

David, who became a man of great courage, stated that he had great fears at one time in his life. Through God, however, he overcame them all: "I sought the Lord, and he heard me, and delivered me from all my fears" (Psalms 34:4). How did David overcome his fears? By merely praying, "Lord, please take away my fears"? Well, he did pray—"I sought the Lord"—but he also did his part in the practical, down-to-earth sense by rising up to choose, to speak, to do what God had taught him to do. Only by this brave personal cooperation did he gain the first cautious victories over his fears. After that, he gradually grew more and more confident of God's help, slaying first the lion and the bear, then Goliath and the Philistines. Thus he became established as a man of boldness.

God wants to do this with us. He wants to deliver us from our fears, establish us in trust, and then increase our confidence until we're as bold as David: "The people that do know their God shall be strong, and do exploits" (Daniel 11:32b). But our deliverance road is the same as that taken by David. We, too, must face our fears in the name of the Lord. No man can gain the upper hand over fear unless he's willing to go face-to-face with the people, situations, or issues that have intimidated him—and with God's help overcome them. Jacob had to face Esau, Samuel had to tell all to Eli, Peter had to receive Gentiles in the presence of the Judaizers. There was no other way for them to "stand fast in the liberty" wherewith Christ had set them free (Galatians 5:1).

Never sit down and quit because you have fears. So does everyone else. Many prominent historical figures have reached heights of greatness from timid, trembling beginnings: "Though thy beginning was small, yet thy latter end should greatly increase" (Job 8:7). Ulysses S. Grant, who became a bold, successful military leader, grew to valor from a very shaky start. He wrote that, when leading his first attack against Confederate forces during the Civil War, he realized he lacked "the moral courage to halt and consider what to do." Upon finding the enemy camp abandoned, he realized that the Confederate commanding officer "had been as much afraid of me as I had been of him." After this, he "never experienced trepidation upon confronting any enemy, though I always felt more or less anxiety."

Evidently Grant learned to *press through* his anxious feelings rather than surrender to them. This apparently minor correction in his attitude made a major difference in the man. The timid, green officer began to grow more confident. And his confidence kept growing until he became a bold, proven general with an impressive string of victories behind him.

Without courage, there can be no revival. When Ezra returned to Jerusalem, he found the Jews backslidden (Ezra 9-10). They needed reviving badly. Then came God's call through Shecaniah: "Arise; for this matter belongeth unto thee . . . be of good courage, and do it" (Ezra 10:4). If God's people were to be revived, Ezra had to lead them through a painful process of divorce. They had to put away their foreign wives and children to comply with God's Law and preserve the purity of the chosen people. Ezra realized that the people might easily rebel against this bitter domestic upheaval. That would mean violent opposition and persecution for the reform movement and its leaders. No doubt he weighed all these things in his mind. But being the man that he was, Ezra overruled his fears, put God's will before his own comfort and safety, and proceeded to deal with the nation's sin. With these necessary reforms in progress, the foundation for revival was properly laid. Then God could send spiritual refreshment in response to the prayers of His righteous remnant.

Without courage, there can be no deliverance. Haman's wicked decree called for the complete extermination of the Jews. At that crucial time, God called upon Esther to act courageously. She was told to intercede before King Ahasuerus for her people (Esther 3-7). Only after she accepted God's stirring challenge through Mordecai did deliverance come. Esther possessed many admirable qualities. She was beautiful, gracious, knowledgeable, discreet, kind, obedient, and faithful. But none of these characteristics brought deliverance. It was her courage that saved the Jewish nation. It was her courage that brought her through the crisis. It was her courage that the Holy Spirit immortalized in Holy Writ with these words: "So will I go in unto the King . . . and if I perish, I perish" (4:16).

Without courage, there can be no fulfillment of divine promises. God led the Israelites out of Egyptian bondage with wonderful promises of a new, fruitful land soon to be theirs. But there was one condition. One very big condition. They had to *take* the land God had given. Canaan would not fall into their hands like ripe figs off a tree; they would have to do battle with the inhabitants of the land: "The violent take it by force" (Matthew 11:12)—"And every man presseth into it" (Luke 16:16). That, of course, required courage.

But the men of Moses' generation shrank from this task and never entered in. By their steady refusal to be courageous they etched the word "coward" on their grave markers and contentedly died in fear, never having enjoyed the blessings God so clearly promised. They *took* nothing. And because they took nothing, they received nothing.

The men of Joshua's generation, however, overcame their fears. In faith, they waged war and won. Doing battle with the experienced Canaanite warriors was no easy thing. Three times in the first chapter of the Book of Joshua, God exhorted Joshua to be courageous: "Be strong and of good courage; for unto this people shalt thou divide for an inheritance the land which I swore unto their fathers to give them" (Joshua 1:6)—"Only be thou strong and very courageous" (1:7)—"Have not I commanded thee? Be strong and of good courage; be not afraid, neither be thou dismayed; for the Lord thy God is with thee whithersoever thou goest" (1:9).

Joshua and his men accepted God's challenge. They endured a series of deadly conflicts and suffered losses. But in the end, they prevailed. They possessed the blessed promised land, not only because of God's help, but because of their own courage. They reached out and *took* all that God offered.

Without courage, we cannot break through the barriers that confront us periodically in the way of righteousness. Although our lives are often uneventful, occasionally a crisis will arise. Satan stands up against us. Some great trouble challenges us, demanding that we stop and give it our undivided attention. Like a mountain it blocks us from going forward (Mark 11:23). We cannot go around it. We must either press through it or turn back in defeat. In such times, we must summon courage. If we hedge, our cowardliness will overrule our courageousness. Everything God is doing in us, for us, and through us will grind to a halt. Not because of our enemy, but because of our sinfully weak reaction to him. We will begin to stagnate like the Israelites and wander through the listless wasteland of lukewarmness.

In the day we stand before Christ, the inexcusable timidity of the saints will be found to have been more damaging to God's cause than the combined efforts of demons, sinners, workers of iniquity, impostors, and false prophets.

One of the most paralyzing fears we have is the fear of reproach. God has commanded us, "Fear not the reproach of men, neither be afraid of their revilings" (Isaiah 51:7-8). Yet most believers are constantly terrorized by thoughts of how others will react if we dare to obey God. What will they say? What will they do? Will they criticize and find fault? Will family and friends oppose us, neighbors avoid us, and fellow believers misjudge us? Will we be laughed at, mocked, and written off as fools? Will our good name be cast out as evil and our reputation ruined?

Such thoughts as these are common to us all. They are our real enemies. They are the giants that keep us out of our promised land—the demons that quench our courage, halt our obedience, and spoil our joy. They are the mountains that block us from going on unto perfection. We must take these fears captive, *press through them,* overcome them. For "the fear of man bringeth a snare" (Proverbs 29:25). Either we snare our thoughts or they snare us. We stop them or they stop us. It's the Canaanites versus the Israelites all over again. It's our personal Kadesh-Barnea (Numbers 13 & 14). We cross over into mature Christian living the day we determine not to give these thoughts place in our minds: "Casting down imaginations . . . and bringing into captivity every thought to the obedience of Christ" (2 Corinthians 10:5).

We're all prone to attacks of cowardice. Timidity may rise up at any time. But, thank God, with Christ and His mighty Spirit within we are also capable of being courageous—if we will only stir ourselves up to it: "Stir up the gift of God, which is in thee" (2 Timothy 1:6).

The natural man of valor relies on himself. He emboldens his soul by remembering his own wisdom, strength, and past victories. Pride prods him forward. Even when scared, he dare not admit to fear lest others hear and mock.

God's bold ones, however, rely not on themselves, but on God's unfailing help. They draw strength by remembering His wisdom, His strength, His past deliverances of His children. The love of God constrains them to face their difficulties bravely for the sake of His name: "Should such a man as I flee?" (Nehemiah 6:11). They dare not disappoint the Christ who saved them: "That he may please him who hath chosen him to be a soldier" (2 Timothy 2:4). Neither do they relish the idea of losing their rich reward in the eternal kingdom to come. Hence, they stand fast before the enemy: "They looked unto him, and were radiant, and their faces were not ashamed" (Psalms 34:5).

Here are some keys for converting cowardice into courage:

Face your fears. When God orders you to do something difficult and fear begins to work on your mind, recognize it for what it is. Don't deny that you're afraid. The first step in getting rid of fear is to acknowledge that you have it. Without this humble basis of truth, God will not help us: "If we confess our sins, he is faithful and just to forgive us our sins, and to cleanse us from all unrighteousness" (1 John 1:9).

Recall God's Word. Remember what God's Word says about fear: "For God hath not given us the spirit of fear, but of power, and of love, and of a sound mind" (2 Timothy 1:7)—"Fear hath torment. He that feareth is not made perfect in love" (1 John 4:18). God's Word alone is the source of faith, and only faith overpowers fear. Soak in the Scriptures that bring God's assurance, peace, and strength straight home to your heart regarding your specific fear-problem.

Cast out fear-thoughts. Get tough with yourself mentally: "Quit you like men, be strong" (1 Corinthians 16:13). Determine to overrule your timidity. Stop considering fearful thoughts and bring your imaginations into captivity to the Word of God, Who so often said, "Fear not." If the Holy Spirit doesn't give fear, fear comes from the opposing spirit—Satan. Then cast it (him) out! Allow the diabolical terrorist no more time or place in the sanctuary of your soul. Keep your mental temple holy: "Perfect love casteth out fear" (1 John 4:18).

Confess your faith. Say to yourself what you believe and what you intend to do with God's help: "I refuse to receive fear in my heart . . . I will not give in to fear . . . The Lord is my helper,

I will not fear." Sincere confession solidifies and establishes faith. Speaking words of agreement with divine truth makes that truth immediately effective in the one who speaks: "Let the redeemed of the Lord say so . . ." (Psalms 107:2).

Act. Whether you feel puny or powerful, make yourself act on what God has shown you. Don't expect to feel strong before you act. Act first, and as you obey God will fill you with His confidence and freedom: "And your joy no man taketh from you" (John 16:22).

Although Samuel "feared to tell Eli the vision," he made himself act (1 Samuel 3:1-18). He spoke out and "told him everything" (3:18). After this action, God established him as a prophet: "And all Israel . . . knew that Samuel was established to be a prophet of the Lord" (3:19-21). Samuel didn't wait for God to establish him before he spoke. He spoke first by faith, without any conscious feeling of confidence; then God strengthened and established him.

But know this. If you hold back after God shows you clearly what to do, fear will always gain the upper hand. The more you hesitate, the stronger your fear will grow, until it completely smothers your spiritual initiative and leaves you weak, defeated, and ashamed: "In thee, O Lord, do I put my trust; let me never be ashamed" (Psalms 31:1).

Here's some good news: *All believers can be equally courageous because of the equally bold One inside of us.* God is with us: "Lo, I am with you always, even unto the end of the age" (Matthew 28:20). God is for us: "If God be for us, who can be against us?" (Romans 8:31). God is in us: "The Lord, thy God in the midst of thee is mighty; he will save" (Zephaniah 3:17). Therefore, if we will only accept every challenge our heavenly Father brings before us in submissive obedience to Him, we cannot fail. Human willingness plus divine ability equals continuously victorious courage.

But if we slink away, hide out, or keep silent, we will surely grieve our Lord: "If any man draw back [from courageous obedience in faith], my soul shall have no pleasure in him" (Hebrews 10:38).

Determine to be among God's brave ones. He never fails to keep, strengthen, and reward the courageous. Whenever God speaks, act! Overrule your fears before they undermine your courage. Then stand fast and wait on your God.

> Fear not; [there is nothing to fear] for I am with you; do not look around you in terror and be dismayed, for I am your God. I will strengthen and harden you [to difficulties]; yes, I will help you; yes, I will hold you up . . .
> (Isaiah 41:10, AMP)

21

God Empowers Those Who Take a Stand!

A long time, therefore, abode they speaking boldly in the Lord, who gave testimony . . . and granted signs and wonders to be done by their hands.

(Acts 14:3)

God lays His power only upon those who take a stand. If we run from the devil's every threat, we abide weak and defeated.

Paul and Barnabas visited the city of Iconium on their first missionary journey. God blessed their evangelistic efforts there, and many souls came into the kingdom of God: "And it came to pass in Iconium that they went both together into the synagogue of the Jews, and so spoke, that a great multitude, both of the Jews and also of the Greeks believed" (Acts 14:1).

But the enemy did not take this sitting down. He stirred up serious trouble for the brethren: "But the unbelieving Jews stirred up the Gentiles, and made their minds evil affected against the brethren" (14:2).

Having many townspeople turn against them, Paul and Barnabas had a crucial decision to make. Should they move on to friendlier territory or stay and continue God's work? Paul chose the latter option. His courage here is noteworthy. It's no easy thing to carry on your work in an environment filled with suspicion, condemnation, and hostility. But Paul knew the enemy's tactics. He learned early in his ministry never to yield to threats. So rather than flee, Paul and Barnabas took a stand: "A long time, therefore, abode they speaking boldly in the Lord" (14:3).

Equally notable is the Lord's response. Paul's resoluteness pleased Him so much that He granted a special anointing of power: "The Lord, who gave testimony unto the word of his grace, and granted signs and wonders to be done by their hands" (14:3).

So we see then that *after* Paul took a stand the Lord empowered him. It wasn't the other way around. The Lord didn't give Paul a conscious influx of spiritual power that inspired him to stay on in a difficult place. No, Paul's courageous choice came first—*then* the Lord strengthened him.

Later on, Paul left Iconium: "And when there was an assault made both of the Gentiles, and also of the Jews with their rulers, to use them despitefully, and to stone them, they were aware of it, and fled unto Lystra and Derbe . . . and there they preached the gospel" (14:5-7). Although their lives were endangered and they are said to have "fled," the apostles did not flee in a spirit of fear or panic. They left only because it was the Lord's time for them to go. He was leading them to depart. There's a time to take a stand and a time to move on: "To every thing there is a season, and a time to every purpose under heaven" (Ecclesiastes 3:1).

Paul and Barnabas obviously had done all they could do among the people of Iconium. If they had left earlier because of the initial change in atmosphere, they would have been failing the Lord, for He still had much work for them to do there. But after they had taken a stand and spent a long time there, God was satisfied with their work. Behind the Jews' plans to assault them was the sovereign hand of God, moving His servants on to their next field of service. As with Job, Paul's assault, although satanic, came forth "from the presence of the Lord" (Job 1:12; 2:7).

There's a saying, "When the going gets tough, the tough get going." God must agree with this philosophy because He frequently arranges tough places for His servants to live or work in. He wants to see which of His children will get going when the going gets tough.

God allowed Jehoshaphat to be surrounded by the armies of hostile neighboring nations (2 Chronicles 20:1-30). But this merely stimulated him to exercise his faith in God. He immediately went into spiritual action, seeking the Lord personally, calling the people together, initiating congregational prayer, instructing and exhorting the people, and obeying God's instructions by taking his stand against his enemies: "Set yourselves, stand ye still . . . tomorrow go out against them" (20:16-17). As Jehoshaphat stood, God strengthened, delivered, and rewarded him.

It was a very tough situation when Sennacherib's army invaded Judah and surrounded the city of Jerusalem (2 Chronicles 32:1-22). So tough, in fact, that

175

it was deadly. But Hezekiah, Isaiah, and the people took a stand against the dreaded power of Assyria and got going by preparing the city's defenses. These daring Judeans called on God for help, trusted in His promise of deliverance, and waited for Him to intervene. For a while, God tested them by allowing their tough situation to remain. The Assyrians camped outside the city walls and Sennacherib's messengers continued to threaten, reproach, and revile the people (32:9-19).

Hezekiah could have fled from this difficulty. He could have compromised with Sennacherib and surrendered, or hastily dispatched a messenger to another nation, asking for military aid. He chose, however, not to run but to stand. As he stood, the power of God enveloped him and held him calmly in place. So strengthened was he that his words comforted and cheered the whole nation in its crisis hour: "And the people rested themselves upon the words of Hezekiah, king of Judah" (32:8).

Not all of God's children react as Jehoshaphat and Hezekiah. When the going gets tough, cowards clear out. As soon as Gideon's army set the battle in array against the Midianites, two thirds of his men left because they were afraid (Judges 7:1-3). They had no intentions of taking a stand. Bondage or no bondage, they were not going to take a risk for the cause of God. At the first opportunity, they went back the way they had come.

Which of these two reactions will we choose?

Some of us have never known what it is to be strengthened and upheld by God because we have refused to take stands for Him when and where we were supposed to. When things become uncomfortable, we conveniently make an exit. That's not God's way. If He should happen to call you away from a difficult setting, by all means obey Him. But many times the call we hear is not the voice of the Spirit, but the voice of our timidity. We get scared and nervous and self-conscious and spurt out of the place God puts us in. And in so doing, we miss out on everything He wants to do for us there in the difficult place—the works, the revelations, the joys, the new strength. Because we opt to flee, He cannot strengthen us.

God wants us to stop running away from our fears. It's time to take a stand. It's time to believe in something and stand for something—time to be uncompromising in our loyalty to Jesus' Words— time to call evil, evil; and good, good—time to speak up for the right and speak out against the evil. God seeks saints who dare to be different, different from the world that knows not God and different from the lukewarm Church that dares not be different. The United States Marine Corps is looking for a "few good men." Where are God's few bold saints?

To take a stand is *not* to start a fight. It's simply to *hold our position and refuse to be moved by the various pressures our antagonists bring to bear on us.* The Spirit exhorts us to "put on the whole armor of God" and "stand against the wiles of the devil" (Ephesians 6:11), but He doesn't tell us to attack our enemies. When we take our stand, our enemies begin to fight against us. Then we must remember to hold our position, but avoid personal retaliation: "Recompense to no man evil for evil" (Romans 12:17). If we fight, we don't stand—if we stand, we don't need to fight, because God fights for us. And if God fights for us, eventually we win: "Sit thou at my right hand, until I make thine enemies thy footstool" (Psalms 110:1).

This is one of the fundamental reasons that the Church at large is glaringly void of spiritual power. God's people are running scared. All the enemy has to do is use his old familiar threats and the sons of God are put to flight. We're intimidated much too easily—we're afraid of offending evildoers; afraid of what people will think, say, or do; afraid that friends and brethren will not stand by us or that our Lord will not deliver as promised. So rather than take a stand, most Christians, when pressured by real or imaginary threats, simply cave in and flee for their lives. Rather than stand still and do the will of God come what may, they take the first available door out of their difficulty, anything to take the pressure off.

These serve not the Lord, but self. Every decision is determined by self-advantage or self-preservation. The path of least resistance may bring quick earthly relief, but it will never lead to eternal glory in God's kingdom. Our Lord taught that Christians who seek to preserve their earthly lives from disruption or loss will, in the end, lose everything—while those who, when tested, risk everything to do His will, will gain everything (Matthew 10:39; Luke 14:25-33; John 12:24; Philippians 3:17-19). The meek will inherit the earth, not self-servers.

Can the Lord send power from on high upon us in this present low state? No, not at all. Paul's experience in Iconium teaches us clearly that we must take a stand to receive God's strength. He only empowers the courageous. If we would just be still and choose to put our trust in God, the pressure would go and wisdom, grace, and power would soon come in its place. Often the pressure we mistake for satanic resistance is really divine insistence. It's God's hand gently but firmly constraining us to take a stand.

The early Church was quite different. They took stands frequently. When the Sanhedrin attempted to quench their message with a religious gag order, the infant saints were forced to a decision. The enemy was attempting to stand them down, to snuff out the truth and drive them out of Jerusalem. It was time to either flee or stand. Their decision was remarkable. Rather than pray for the Lord to take away the threat that hung over their heads, they prayed for strength to stand strong under its weight: "And now, Lord, behold their threatenings; and grant unto thy servants, that with all boldness they may speak thy word, by stretching forth thine hand to heal; and that signs and wonders may be done by the name of thy holy child, Jesus" (Acts 4:29-30). The Lord was deeply pleased and immediately granted their request: "And when they had prayed, the place was shaken where they were assembled together; and they were all filled with the Holy Spirit, and they spoke the word of God with boldness" (Acts 4:31).

When the disciples took their stand, the Jews promptly took a counterstand—and threw them in jail: "Then the high priest rose up, and all they that were with him . . . and laid their hands on the apostles, and put them in the common prison" (Acts 5:17-18). At this crucial point, the Lord sent His sorely-tried followers a rather surprising message. He told them to defy the false religious authorities and take yet *another* stand: "Go, stand and speak in the temple to the people all the words of this life" (Acts 5:20). And they did just that: "And when they heard that, they entered into the temple early in the morning, and taught" (5:21).

We will find the same thing true today. When we take a stand in God, worldlings and false brethren take a counterstand against us. It's then that the Lord stands by us to strengthen us and see us through to the end. His divine aid is always sufficient, with or without additional human support: "At my first defense no man stood with me, but all men forsook me . . . Notwithstanding, the Lord stood with me and strengthened me, that by me the preaching might be fully known" (2 Timothy 4:16-17). But the Lord can't stand by us while we're running away. When Elijah fled in terror from Jezebel's threat, he soon became exhausted and collapsed under a juniper tree (1 Kings 19:1-4). If we want God's presence to strengthen us, we must stop running and stand still in trust and call our enemy's bluff.

Those who take a stand encourage others to take a stand. They become spiritual role models. Their courage becomes contagious, spreading from saint to saint. Moses' bold stand before Pharaoh encouraged his brethren to tough out those last difficult days in the slime pits. Jonathan's exploit stirred his frightened brethren to come out of hiding and overcome the enemy. David's stand against Goliath encouraged Israel's other soldiers to face the battle. Paul's sturdiness amid his bonds and afflictions emboldened many to preach with a conviction they had never known before: "And many of the brethren in the Lord, becoming confident by my bonds, are much more bold to speak the word without fear" (Philippians 1:14). John's lonely stand on Patmos no doubt encouraged other suffering disciples scattered throughout Asia to stand firm and endure their share of the afflictions of the gospel.

Brethren, may God smite us with sickness. Not a harmful, physical disease, but a godly, spiritual grief, a "godly sorrow" that "worketh repentance" (2 Corinthians 7:10). In laymen's language, may we become so sick of our inexcusable timidity that we actually do something about it—that the next time God puts us in a difficult place we decide to take a stand and trust the Lord to strengthen and keep us. And may we hold our ground until He leads us to move on. If enough of us decide to take on this philosophy, it may result in nothing short of *Pentecost II*. For as surely as God is God, if we take the stands He bids us take, He will send His power down upon us.

> Stand fast, therefore, in the liberty with which Christ hath made us free, and be not entangled again with the yoke of bondage.
>
> (Galatians 5:1)
>
> Always laboring fervently for you in prayers, that ye may stand perfect and complete in all the will of God.
>
> (Colossians 4:12)

Having done all . . . stand. Stand, therefore,
having your loins girded about with truth . . .
(Ephesians 6:13 -14)

22

When the Clash Comes

*If any man come to me, and hate not his
father, and mother, and wife, and children, and
brethren, and sisters, yea, and his own life also,
he cannot be my disciple.*

(Luke 14:26)

Referring to Luke 14:26, the *Ryrie Study Bible*
states: "This saying does not justify malice or ill will
toward one's family, but it means that devotion to
family must take second place to one's devotion to
Christ."

Walter Beuttler taught, "No natural claim, no
earthly possession, no kind of a relationship or
attachment to things or persons, can be allowed to
stand between us and the call of God, if we are
indeed to 'follow Him.'"

The *Modern Language Bible* (New Berkeley
Version) notes: "Terms that express emotions are
sometimes comparative and this must be the case in

183

this instance. In a clash of claims, Jesus must be first and everything and everyone else have a lesser claim."

It's vitally important that aspiring Christian disciples understand that occasionally clashes will occur between God's will and others' will for us; also between God's will and our own will for ourselves. At such times, we must hate—that is, deliberately disregard—every claim that competes against the Master's will. Our lives are Christ's and not our own: "What? Know ye not that . . . ye are not your own? For ye are bought with a price; therefore, glorify God in your body and in your spirit, which are God's" (1 Corinthians 6:19-20). Therefore, Christ alone must rule us, not self or other people. We must allow Him to command our every step without interference from well-meaning friends, relatives, or Christian brethren—or from our own sanctified intelligence: "Lean not to thine own understanding" (Proverbs 3:5-6).

The call of God is strictly an individual matter. God calls each one of us separately and apart from others. At times, the path He calls us to take seems reasonable to others. They smile and give their nod of approval. But at other times, the Spirit calls us to go in a way they simply cannot understand. Why? Because the natural mind can't understand and therefore doesn't accept the ways and means of the Spirit of God: "But the natural man receiveth not the things of the Spirit of God; for they are foolishness unto him, neither can he know them, because they are spiritually discerned" (1 Corinthians 2:14).

This creates an awkward situation. The disciple cannot explain to other people the way the Lord is leading Him. Why? Because often, he doesn't understand it himself. The Lord requires us to trust and obey His call without a detailed explanation on His part. He calls us to walk by faith, not by reason as we did formerly. We must obey His initiatives without knowing what our obedience will lead to and how God will work everything out: "What I do thou knowest not now, but thou shalt know hereafter" (John 13:7). We must walk in the steps of the father of our faith, Abraham, who "by faith . . . obeyed; and he went out, not knowing whither he went" (Hebrews 11:8).

At this crucial point, aware of our dilemma, Jesus draws near. As we meditate in the Scriptures, He speaks and assures us with words that in effect say, "Child, fear not. Take the path I set before you. I will go before you, strengthen you, give you wisdom and counsel, and open up My perfect plan before you as you take each step in obedient faith."

Inspired by this assurance, we take our first step in obedience to His call. When we do, immediately the clash comes.

Our family protests. Father says, "That's ridiculous. You're being fanatical; you must be deceived." Mother says, "Aren't you taking a big risk?" Wife or husband says, "Oh, that could never be God's will for you. You're just not suited for that." The children join in the clamor, "No, no, we want you home more. Don't you love us?" Our natural brothers and sisters complain, "We don't see you much any more. Where have you been keeping yourself? You're not taking that religion of yours too seriously, are you?" Then our fellow Christians begin to voice their disapproval: "What's wrong with you? Why are you doing that? The Lord hasn't called any of us that way. Why you? Who do you think you are?"

And finally, after all these outside voices have spoken, we hear opposition from within. Our self-life objects strenuously: "If I do this, what will I do for money? And who will help with this task, that responsibility, this need? What will I meet with after I obey?"

Thus far, God has called and other claims have clashed with that call. The question, though difficult, is now clear: Are we going to be true disciples of Christ or not?

His instructions in Luke 14:26-27 teach us what we must do. When the clash comes, we must hate all other claims, accept our personal cross, and follow on faithfully in the footsteps of our misunderstood Master. If we don't, we cannot be a true disciple: "Whosoever doth not bear his cross, and come after me, cannot be my disciple" (14:27). There is no middle ground. We either heed the call or succumb to the clash.

When confronted with this painful decision, we may take comfort in the fact that the one who calls us to take up our cross has taken up His own before us. Jesus did the will of His Father while possessionless (Matthew 8:20), while His mother misunderstood Him (Luke 2:50; 8:19-21), while His brothers hated and mocked Him (John 7:1-9), while His friends thought Him to be insane (Mark 3:21), and while the members of His own synagogue rejected His preaching and tried to put Him to death (Luke 4:28-30). We will never experience any personal grief that He has not experienced, so we may go to Him for comfort in all our afflictions. To some degree, every true disciple reenacts the way He went—that is, "outside the camp, bearing his reproach" (Hebrews 13:13).

But discipleship remains optional. Jesus doesn't make us take up our cross and follow Him. If we prefer, we may hate the cross. Thousands of Christians do: "For many . . . are enemies of the cross of Christ" (Philippians 3:18-19). We may ignore Christ's claims and go back to the nominal Christian lifestyle to keep people happy with us. But if we do, we will never be genuine disciples. Saved? Yes. But committed disciples, sold-out students of Jesus Christ? No. And all our lives, we will be haunted by the memory of our spiritual failure.

Many Christians today suffer painful flashbacks of their personal Kadesh-Barnea, the time and place where they came to the very border of the purpose of God for their lives, looked upon it, touched it, tasted it, and then turned back from what God was plainly impelling them to do. And why? Because of the clash. Because of the fear of man: "The fear of man bringeth a snare" (Proverbs 29:25). The opinions and praises of men meant more to them than the Lord's approval: "For they loved the praise of men more than the praise of God" (John 12:43). So to please them, they displeased Him: "Wherefore, I was grieved with that generation" (Hebrews 3:10).

In Luke 14:25-35, Jesus foretells the end of believers who refuse to pay the high cost of discipleship. They will eventually be mocked by the very people whose approval they so carefully sought to gain: "This man began to build, and was not able to finish" (14:28-30). They will compromise and make peace with the very enemies God called them to confront and overcome: "While the other is yet a great way off, he sendeth an embassy, and desireth conditions of peace" (14:31-32). They will be as worthless to God as tasteless salt is to men: "Salt is good; but if the salt have lost its savor" (14:34). Even dung will have more value in God's sight than a believer who turns back from His high calling: "It is neither fit . . . for the dunghill" (14:35).

Truly, the cost of New Testament discipleship is real and it is great. At one time or another God will test disciples over every possession and relationship they have: "Whosoever he is of you that forsaketh not all that he hath, cannot be my disciple" (14:33). But when the clash comes in your life, remember this important and repeatedly proven fact: *Though the immediate cost of obedience to God's call is great, the cost of disobedience will ultimately be much greater.* What befell Lot is clear proof of that (Genesis 19:14b, 26, 30-38).

When God calls, go with Him and burn your bridges behind you. Consider only the way your Master went and the sacrifices of others who have borne their crosses before you: "For consider him that endured such contradictions of sinners against himself" (Hebrews 12:3).

Always heed the call, never the clash.

23

A Matrimonial Message

Then Zipporah . . . said, Surely a bloody husband art thou to me.

(Exodus 4:25)

Heaven-sent marriages are not always heavenly. But they are always intended to serve heavenly purposes.

Through Reuel, God providentially chose Zipporah to be Moses' wife: "And Moses was content to dwell with the man; and he gave Moses Zipporah, his daughter" (Exodus 2:21). Yet Exodus 4:24-26 reveals that she was unruly, contentious, and without respect for Moses or his God. Her grievous faults must have made Moses wonder whether a place much farther below had arranged for his matrimonial mess. However, although his marriage to Zipporah was not the happily-ever-after kind, it was indeed ordained of God for His supreme purpose.

The inspired record of what occurred by the way in the inn is more than a brief accounting of an isolated incident in Moses' life. *It's a revelation of what his forty-year marriage to Zipporah was like.* Zipporah's words and actions on that well-known occasion betray her deep faults. Let's examine them.

"A bloody husband thou art, because of the circumcision" (4:26). Zipporah was unruly. She refused to bow her knee to Moses' God. It was God, not Moses, who had decreed that all of Abraham's seed must be circumcised (Genesis 17:9-14). In refusing to permit her second son to be circumcised prior to Moses' critical illness, Zipporah was living in full, conscious defiance of God and His holy Word. A "meek and quiet spirit" (1 Peter 3:4) she had not.

"Surely a bloody husband art thou to me . . . a bloody husband thou art" (4:25-26). Zipporah was also contentious. Contentious people love to keep bringing up controversial matters, even when no chance for agreement exists. They love to strive about words to no profit. They delight in repeating themselves persistently on matters not open for discussion.

Note that Zipporah spewed out her famous reproach, "Surely, a bloody husband art thou to me," not once but twice. She made the statement first when she had just finished circumcising Eliezer (14:25). But lambasting Moses once did not satisfy her. So she blasted him a second time while he was recovering from his illness (14:26). The Book of Proverbs speaks of the unpleasantness of dwelling "with a brawling woman in a wide house" (Proverbs 21:9). Moses evidently knew all about this. Zipporah was a prime example of a "contentious woman" (Proverbs 27:15).

"Then Zipporah took a sharp stone and cut off the foreskin of her son, and cast it at his feet" (14:25).

Zipporah's rude gesture here—throwing her son's bloody foreskin at Moses' feet—testifies to her lack of respect for her husband. And she showed no remorse for her contemptuous act. No mention is made of any apology. She obviously was accustomed to belittling Moses.

"So he let him go; then Zipporah . . . said, Surely a bloody husband art thou" (14:26). Zipporah had no mercy. At least she had none for Moses. Still recovering from a deadly illness, Moses needed peace and quiet. It was neither the time nor the place for a disagreement. But void of compassion, Zipporah tried to ignite an argument anyway.

To strike a wounded man is a mark of the lowest sort of character. Verbally, Zipporah did this very thing. Instead of lovingly nursing God's deliverer back to health, she added to his sorrow by railing at him.

The most serious charge against Zipporah is that she sought to turn Moses away from God. It's implied here that the subject of circumcision had been discussed in Moses' home previously. Moses suggested it, Zipporah opposed it, and that ended that. Moses, of course, was entirely to blame for yielding to his wife's ungodly counsel in this matter. God made that quite clear when He sought to kill *Moses*, not Zipporah. Nevertheless, by opposing her husband's desire to obey God, Zipporah was encouraging him to disobey God. She was seeking to put a wedge between Moses and God. Originally given to Moses' helper, Zipporah turned out to be his constant hindrance and a thorn in his flesh.

191

It's clear then that Moses' heaven-sent marriage was far from heavenly. Nevertheless, it wrought God's designated purpose in him. Didn't God know what Zipporah would turn out to be? Of course. Why then did He ordain her marriage to his handpicked leader? Because in learning to live with Zipporah, Moses was preparing himself to lead the children of Israel, who later proved to be every bit as unruly, disrespectful, and contentious as Zipporah. Forty years with Zipporah readied Moses for forty years with the Israelites.

And, except for the matter of Eliezer's circumcision, Moses did learn how to consistently overcome Zipporah's difficult nature. If he had not, God would never have sent him back to Egypt to deliver his brethren. God's release and blessing of Moses after settling the circumcision issue proves that no other disobedience remained in his life.

During the long, difficult years that followed the Exodus, Moses was often tempted and tried by the Israelites. They were so petty, so small, so self-centered. They refused to trust God, complained about everything, resisted Moses and Aaron, and drew back when God wanted to bless them. They were amazingly vexatious. How was Moses able to respond as graciously and patiently as he did? How was he able to overcome their relentless provocations? Why did he constantly forgive and intercede instead of reject them? (Numbers 14:10-20; 21:5-9). *Because he had learned to do the same thing during his forty years with Zipporah.* She had often acted the same way. In learning to overcome her difficult nature, Moses had unconsciously prepared himself to rule over the Israelites. His painful personal life, therefore, was God's workshop in which He made Moses after His will. It was a cross experience, a death, that afterwards led to a personal resurrection of fruitful service and the deliverance of multitudes.

So God's heavenly purpose of raising up a strong, spiritually minded leader was wrought after all, even in the midst of a less-than-heavenly marriage.

The *Amplified Bible* (AMP) has a notation on 1 Samuel 25:31 that states: "In *Through the Bible Day by Day*, F. B. Meyer said, 'Never let the evil disposition of one mate hinder the devotion and grace of the other. Never let the difficulties of your home lead you to abdicate your throne. Do not step down to the level of your circumstances, but lift them to your own high calling in Christ.'"

Like Moses, your marriage may be far from ideal. You may live with a Zipporah or a Michal (2 Samuel 6:12-23). Or you may be an Abigail married to a Nabal (1 Samuel 25). Your situation could even conceivably be worse. Whatever the difficulties of your home life, remember what God did in Moses in the midst of a difficult marriage. Let Him duplicate His purpose in your life. Moses' marriage was not easy, but God meant it unto good to bring forth a mature soul who could, like Joseph, "save many people alive" (Genesis 50:20).

The God that wrought wondrously in Moses is waiting to do the same in you. But your attitude is the key. If you rebel against the difficulty and stop walking with God, you will be no deliverer. But if you see your marital difficulties from the spiritual viewpoint and obey God closely yourself, you will emerge from *your* Midian experience strong, merciful, and spiritually minded. And God will use you to strengthen and deliver many others.

> And we know that all things work together for good to them that love God, to them who are the called according to His purpose . . . to be conformed to the image of his Son.
>
> (Romans 8:28-29)

24

He Wounds and He Heals

See now that I, even I, am he . . . I wound,
and I heal.

(Deuteronomy 32:39)

At times, God finds it necessary to wound souls in order to bring His redemptive purposes to pass in the earth. But the hand that wounds also heals: ". . . I wound, and I heal . . ." (Deuteronomy 32:39).

By the Spirit, Simeon informed Mary that she must experience deep personal sorrow in order that many might be given repentance and salvation: "And Simeon blessed them, and said unto Mary, his mother . . . (Yea, a sword shall pierce through thy own soul also), that the thoughts of many hearts may be revealed" (Luke 2:34-35). This sword period lasted from the beginning of Jesus' ministry until His post-resurrection appearances. During that interim, Mary's heart was pierced repeatedly by misunderstanding, perplexity, and sorrow. When Jesus went forth to fulfill His "Father's business" (Luke 2:49)—His miraculous ministry and sacrificial death—Mary simply could not understand. Her motherly love was slain so that God's fatherly love might adopt many children. Her family was divided so that God's family might be established and united. Her way of life was closed so that God could open a new and living way for all who believe. A sacrifice had to be made. And God sovereignly chose to lay it on *Mary*. If the world was to be permanently healed, she had to be temporarily wounded: "Yea, a sword shall pierce through thy own soul also."

As Jesus' mother, Mary was His closest natural relative. And His difficult and fruitful ministry caused her to suffer greatly. This tells us that *those most closely related to God's chosen servants must at times suffer greatly so that God's eternal fruit may be brought forth.*

What exactly did Mary suffer? What caused her sorrows, her piercing sword? Mary's sufferings sprang from Christ's sufferings. She suffered as she watched Him suffer. When we love someone, a line of communication exists between us and that person by which all emotional impulses are shared. When they feel joy, we feel joy—when they are hurt, we hurt. This was the case with Mary. She suffered empathetically. Everything that was done and said against Jesus, Mary felt and suffered along with Him: "The reproaches of those who reproached thee are fallen upon me" (Psalms 69:9).

In the Spirit, Simeon characterized Jesus' upcoming ministry as "a sign which shall be spoken against" (Luke 2:34). How true were his words! As Jesus' ministry grew, so did the rumors, misunderstandings, false representations, and wild accusations. Some of these were caused by the people's ignorance, but others were due to the deliberate and spiteful slander campaign of the scribes and Pharisees: "Then again called they the man that was blind, and said unto him, Give God the praise; we know that this man is a sinner" (John 9:24)—"And there was much murmuring among the people concerning him; . . . others said, Nay, but he deceiveth the people" (John 7:12)—"And the scribes who came down from Jerusalem said, He hath Beelzebub, and by the prince of the demons casteth he out demons" (Mark 3:22). Mary heard all these false reports, and, knowing Jesus' true character, they grieved her deeply.

Jesus' two visits to Nazareth make it clear that He was highly unpopular in His hometown: "And they were offended at him" (Mark 6:3). The townspeople tried to assassinate Him: "And all they in the synagogue . . . were filled with wrath, and rose up, and thrust him out of the city, and led him unto the brow of the hill on which their city was built, that they might cast him down headlong" (Luke 4:28-29). Even His own brothers mocked Him: "His brethren, therefore, said unto him, Depart from here, and go into Judea, that thy disciples also may see the works that thou doest. For there is no man that doeth anything in secret, and he himself seeketh to be known openly. If thou do these things, show thyself to the world. For neither did his brethren believe in him" (John 7:3-5).

Whenever Jesus visited Nazareth, He suffered strong rejection. But His suffering there was only temporary. Soon He left to preach in other cities. When He left, however, Mary remained. While

Jesus "went about all Galilee, teaching in their synagogues, and preaching the gospel of the kingdom" (Matthew 4:23), Mary stayed behind in Nazareth. Living there among the friends, family, and acquaintances who greatly misunderstood and rejected her son's actions, she undoubtedly felt the sharp edge of the sword daily: "And when his friends heard of it . . . they said, He is beside himself" (Mark 3:21). To make things worse, Mary couldn't answer for Jesus. How could she explain Jesus satisfactorily to her fellow Nazarenes when she didn't fully understand Him herself? How could she give them answers that she didn't have?

Mary's sword reached its climax when Jesus was tried, mocked, beaten, and crucified. John 19:25 reveals that Mary stood by the Cross when the end came: "Now there stood by the cross of Jesus his mother." The sword's final thrust occurred at Calvary: "But one of the soldiers, with a spear, pierced his side" (John 19:34). When the soldier's spear pierced Jesus' bloodied body, God's sword of sorrow pierced Mary's battered soul—for the last time. It was all over then. God returned His sword to its sheath. The furious hatred, the lies, the scandal, the envious opposition of the religious leaders, the local and national rejection—all of this terrible wounding—ceased.

Soon afterward, God began to heal Mary's wounds: "To every thing there is a season, and a time to every purpose under the heaven . . . a time to heal" (Ecclesiastes 3:1, 3). He arranged circumstances so that Mary was in the upper room along with the apostles and the other disciples, awaiting the coming of the Holy Spirit: "And when they were come in, they went up into an upper room, where abode Peter, and James, and John . . . These all continued with one accord in prayer and supplication, with the women, and Mary, the mother of Jesus, and with his brethren" (Acts 1:12-14). After Mary received the fullness of the Spirit, all the things she had pondered in her heart in days gone by suddenly made sense. Like the pieces of a confusing puzzle coming together, she began to get the full picture. Jesus really was the Son of God, the long-awaited Messiah, Jehovah God in human flesh. Now she had no doubts, no gaps in her understanding.

The rest of Mary's life was spent in joyful fellowship with her own sons, James and Jude, who were recently converted by an appearance by the Lord, and with John, in whose home she resided (John 19:25-27). After three years of ceaseless wounding, the God-ordained time of healing that followed was a blessed relief—days of heaven on earth, days filled full of Spirit-illuminated conversation and apostolic fellowship. In the end, Mary felt no hurt. Her healing was complete, her joy full.

The Scriptures tell us of others who also experienced wounding and healing by God.

Joseph was a very fruitful servant of the Lord: "Joseph is a fruitful bough, even a fruitful bough by a well" (Genesis 49:22). The heart of his father, Jacob, was pierced on the day he was informed of Joseph's supposed death (Genesis 37:31-33). The patriarchs' report was a lie, of course, but Jacob's psychological suffering was real and intense. Joseph's body had not truly been rent. But Jacob's soul was torn apart with inconsolable sorrow: "And Jacob tore his clothes, and put sackcloth upon his loins, and mourned for his son many days. And all of his sons and all his daughters rose up to comfort him; but he refused to be comforted; and he said, For I will go down into Sheol unto my son mourning. Thus his father wept for him" (Genesis 37:34-35). Jacob's wound, the sword that pierced his heart, continued until his joyful reunion with Joseph in Egypt some twenty-two years later (Genesis 46:29-30).

Then God's healing process began. Jacob and the patriarchs spent seventeen fruitful and prosperous years in Goshen, "the best of the land" of Egypt (Genesis 47:6, 27-28). It was a sweet and fitting end to a bitter story. God wounded, but then He healed. And in his latter days Jacob felt no hurt.

As Christians, we may as well face the facts. If we obey God's call, some who are close to us will undoubtedly be hurt. The sword will visit and pierce them through: "Think not that I am come to send peace on earth; I came not to send peace, but a sword" (Matthew 10:34). As those who love us watch us suffer, they will suffer. Because they cannot understand us, they will worry. Because they cannot explain our actions to others, they will hurt. Because we continue to pursue the strait and narrow way, they will cry out in protest.

Others may suffer for opposing us. They may judge us, belittle our faith and fight against us bitterly: "A man's foes shall be they of his own household" (Matthew 10:36). They may deliberately misrepresent us and betray us: "And ye shall be betrayed both by parents, and brethren, and kinsfolk, and friends" (Luke 21:16). They may try to harm us: "And the brother shall deliver up the brother to death, and the father the child; and the children shall rise up against their parents" (Matthew 10:21). For this evil, God may chasten them sore. They may slowly self-destruct before our eyes—mentally, emotionally, physically—almost to the point of death.

But know this. If we will go steadily forward doing our Father's business like our Master, the day will come when the hand that wounded will also heal. The sword will depart and the salve will come in its stead—a supernatural balm to heal every wound and restore every joy. God will wipe away all tears and fill our mouths with laughter. He did this for Jesus. His mother and brothers were converted and gathered in with the disciples. He did this for Joseph. His father was blessed and his brothers spared. And He did this for Job: "And the Lord turned the captivity of Job . . . Then came there unto him all his brethren, and all his sisters, and all they that had been of his acquaintance before, and did eat bread with him in his house, and they bemoaned him, and comforted him over all the evil that the Lord had brought upon him" (Job 42:10-11).

When God's time of healing comes, it will be so complete, so wonderful, so exceedingly abundantly above our limited expectations, that we will forget the wounding and the sorrow: "For God, said he, hath made me forget" (Genesis 41:51)—"because the former troubles are forgotten" (Isaiah 65:16).

> For he maketh sore, and bindeth up; he woundeth, and his hands make whole.
>
> (Job 5:18)

25

Thinning the Ranks

From that time, many of his disciples went
back, and walked no more with him.

(John 6:66)

As quoted above, at one point in Jesus' ministry,
"many of his disciples went back, and walked no
more with him." Why did they go back? The
complete story recorded in the sixth chapter of
John's Gospel gives us the answer.

In Capernaum, two groups accompanied Jesus.
There were the larger multitude of His "disciples"
that followed Him from city to city throughout
Israel, hearing His words, witnessing His works, and
looking for His kingdom (6:66). Then there were
"the twelve" (6:67), His smaller, handpicked circle
of constant companions whom He later empowered
and sent forth as special messengers. The twelve
were not fly-by-night types. Having "left all" to
follow Jesus (Mark 10:28), they were in His camp for

the long haul. Sink or swim, win or lose, kingdom or no kingdom, they were with Him.

The other disciples, however, were distinctly less committed. They followed Him when He miraculously healed the sick: "And a great multitude followed him, because they saw his miracles which he did on those who were diseased" (John 6:2). They followed Him when He multiplied the bread and fish to feed them (6:5-14). They followed Him when He crossed the Sea of Galilee (6:15-24). But when His sayings became hard, they were immediately offended: "This is an hard saying. Who can hear it?" (6:60). They gave up their high hopes, deserted the Nazarene prophet, and returned to the normalcy of their former lives.

What were these hard sayings? This passage (John 6:1-71) and other passages in the New Testament help us understand what they were.

First, they were teachings that were *hard to understand*. Christ's more mystical teachings were difficult for the natural (rationalistic, fleshly) mind to comprehend. When Jesus claimed to be the bread of life, adding that true followers would eat His flesh and drink His blood, the rationalists simply tuned Him out. That was more than they could handle. He was too far up in the clouds for them. They couldn't grasp such ultra-spiritual talk: "But the natural man receiveth not the things of the Spirit of God; for they are foolishness unto him . . ." (1 Corinthians 2:14).

Second, they were teachings that were costly to put into practice, or *hard to carry out*. They are found throughout the four Gospels. Jesus ordered a young, wealthy seeker to give up all his earthly possessions (Luke 18:22-23). He called another man to leave his dying father to go preach the gospel (Luke 9:59-62). He taught that if even the best things hinder our spiritual development, they should be cut out of our lives (Matthew 5:29-30). He warned that true Christianity would split some families right down the middle (Matthew 10:34-39; 12:46-50). None of these demands were easily or lightly obeyed: "Hard is the way which leadeth unto life, and few there be that find it" (Matthew 7:14).

Third, they were sayings that were *hard to accept*. Rebukes and corrections are disillusioning things. We understand them but we don't like them. Our mind grasps them but our pride rises up and throws them out. But since "reproofs of instruction are the way of life" (Proverbs 6:23), God warns us, "Despise not thou the chastening of the Lord" (Hebrews 12:5-15).

The disciples who went back because of Jesus' hard sayings began following Him in Jerusalem, having seen His miracles there (John 6:2). Then He fed them in the wilderness (6:5-14). So impressed were they with this man who could heal the sick and feed the hungry, that they immediately got the idea of rebelling against Roman rule (6:14-15). Jesus was their material solution, the perfect king. They were ready for revolution—right then.

Knowing their thoughts, Jesus immediately took evasive action: "He departed again into a mountain himself alone" (6:15). He would have no part of politics. He was bound for a cross, not a crown. That night, the twelve crossed the Sea of Galilee (6:16-21). Jesus rendezvoused with them in the midst of the sea and they all landed together at Capernaum (6:21).

When the multitude realized that Jesus' disciples were gone, "they also took boats and came to Capernaum, seeking for Jesus" (6:24). And the next day, they found Him (6:25).

What was Jesus' response to this eager multitude? Hard sayings.

First He rebuked them, stating that their motive in seeking Him was all wrong: "Ye seek me . . . because ye did eat of the loaves, and were filled" (6:26). Then He corrected them, stating that they ought to labor for spiritual things with the same zeal they had shown in seeking bread. They had *labored*, rowing across the Sea of Galilee to find Jesus for bread's sake. They should now *labor* for eternal bread, studying God's Word and building their faith: "Labor not for the food which perisheth, but [labor] for that food which endureth unto everlasting life, which the Son of man shall give unto you . . ." (6:27). While they were still smarting from this hard saying, He spoke yet another—one hard to understand— revealing that they should eat His flesh and drink His blood (6:30-65).

All of this taken together was simply too much for many of them. They immediately forsook the Master: "From that time many of his disciples went back" (6:66).

Here's an interesting fact: *The crowd that deserted Jesus in Capernaum was the same crowd that was eager to follow Him in insurrection just the day before.* Christ's hard sayings paralyzed their self-centered religious zeal. Instead of following Him to war, they peacefully forsook Him. Suddenly His army shrank.

Did the Lord blunder by saying these things when He did? Or were they timed intentionally?

Surely the latter is true. For Jesus knew His followers' hearts all along: "For Jesus knew from the beginning who they were that believed" (6:64). He knew that the "bread-disciples" would reject His rebukes and His deeply spiritual teachings.

On another occasion, He did the same thing. Just when great multitudes went with Him, He turned and stated the costly conditions of discipleship (Luke 14:25-33). He knew that the spiritual explosion caused by His bombshell of truth would drive away only those who had not the resolve to follow Him all the way.

The purpose of His hard sayings, therefore, was to test His followers. Their willpower was measured, their motives searched, and their true gods exposed. They were driven to a choice and divided, true from false, sheep from goats, disciples indeed from disciples in word only. Like Gideon's army (Judges 7:1-7), His flock was reduced to its true soldiers. *Out of all the eager thousands that thronged to see Jesus in the height of His ministry, only 120 faithful souls endured to the end—through the Cross to the upper room* (Acts 1:15).

It seems clear, then, that our Lord did not want artificially to increase the number of His followers. To the contrary, He purposely uttered hard sayings to reduce them. He made no effort to win the mixed multitude. Proud, fearful, or self-indulgent recruits would weaken the resolve of His good soldiers. So He refused to enlist those who sought Him only for bread—for selfish desires, materialism, and pleasure: "By the three hundred men who lapped will I save you . . . let all the other people go" (Judges 7:7). Jesus' attitude was that those who wouldn't go all the way should go away. He wanted permanent disciples, those who would follow "wholly" (Joshua 14:8). He would invest His time, toil, and truth in them.

How different our attitude is today. Believing that security lies in large numbers, we worship multitudes. We dilute Jesus' words, alter His image, and market Him to the masses. Anything and everything is said and done to draw people into our organizations with no thought for either the faithfulness of our message or the motives of our converts—or our own motives.

But Christ's hard sayings still test us and thin our ranks.

Of the vast multitudes that today profess Christ, few are willing to follow Him all the way. Most are interested only in the bread—the immediate earthly benefits He bestows. At first, they appear extremely interested in Jesus: "They who, when they hear, receive the word with joy" (Luke 8:13). But when the excitement dies down and Jesus begins saying hard things, one by one they fall away: "And in time of testing fall away" (Luke 8:13). They stop believing, seeking, and fellowshiping, and go back to their former existence.

Has something like this happened in your church? Has the exciting influx of converts ceased and a quiet outflow of backsliders commenced? Have your multitudes become "minitudes." Don't be troubled, your Master is at work: "It is I; be not afraid" (John 6:20). His hard sayings are testing, dividing, purging. He is finding His true remnant: "For there must be also heresies among you, that they who are approved may be made manifest"

(1 Corinthians 11:19). When the inevitable thinning process is over, only divinely-called disciples will remain. *The souls God adds don't go back.*

At the Last Supper, Jesus praised the eleven for their loyalty. They had endured to the end: "Ye are they who have continued with me in my trials" (Luke 22:28). And fifty days later, He rewarded them. They were the first to receive the Holy Spirit, enter into the deeper spiritual walk, receive authority to preach, teach, heal, and deliver, and witness the wondrous visitation. They were glad then that they had not gone back.

We all recognize God's work when our memberships are on the rise. The Lord is surely present when many press into the camp. But this lesson shows us the other side: *He is also at work when many depart.* O yes, Satan is the wolf who seeks to divide and devour the flock. But he can do nothing unless it's given him from above. When churches are declining in membership, boiling in controversy, or being rent asunder by differing beliefs, the Lord is present, thinning the ranks. Let us understand this and be content to company with His faithful few. He would rather have a loyal microchurch than a megachurch filled with seekers of bread.

When the final revival breaks out, we'll be glad we did not go back.

26

Shall He Find This Belief?

. . . Nevertheless, when the Son of Man
cometh, shall he find faith on the earth?

(Luke 18:8)

Jesus' parable of the unjust judge and the persistent widow is more than an important lesson regarding prayer (Luke 18:1-8). It is prophetic. It tells us something about these last days. This is clear from Christ's statement in verse 8: "When the Son of Man cometh, shall He find . . . ?" He implies that conditions similar to those described in the parable will exist when He returns. In their final hour, His true disciples will be persecuted by apostates as the widow was by her adversary, and will seek justice and deliverance from Him.

In this regard, the key word in this parable is "avenge." Note its repeated use: "Avenge me of mine adversary" (18:3)—"I will avenge her" (18:5)—"Shall not God avenge?" (18:7)—"He will avenge" (18:8).

Webster's states that avenge "implies the infliction of deserved or just punishment for wrongs or oppressions." As is seen in this parable, this avenging is properly executed by a higher authority. The woman did not take matters into her own hands. She repeatedly asked the judge to avenge her: "She came unto him, saying, Avenge me" (18:3).

Being avenged, therefore, differs from taking revenge. Revenge is personal retaliation motivated by anger arising from a suffered wrong. Jesus is not advocating revenge. He taught us to "resist not evil" (Matthew 5:39-43).

When evil people persecute us to hinder us from doing God's will, we should patiently and believingly cry to God to avenge us of our adversaries. That is, to intervene and do whatever is necessary to relieve the situation, to send whatever punishment is required to deliver and vindicate us so that His work may go forward. At some point, God must deliver His true servants from their enemies if they are to serve Him freely: "That he would grant unto us that we, being delivered out of the hand of our enemies, might serve him without fear, in holiness and righteousness before him, all the days of our life" (Luke 1:74-75)—"Finally, brethren, pray for us, that the word of the Lord may have free course . . . that we may be delivered from unreasonable and wicked men" (2 Thessalonians 3:1-2). In nearly every Psalm, David cried out against his enemies and expressed confidence that God would deliver him from their hands.

In Christ's parable, the widow has suffered an unspecified injury from an unnamed adversary (18:3). So she seeks justice from the unjust judge who "feared not God, neither regarded man" (18:2). True to his name, this unjust judge refuses to give her justice "for a while" (18:4). But the woman does not "faint" (18:1). She persists and importunes, petitioning the unjust judge daily for justice. Finally, due to sheer irritation and exhaustion, he yields and reverses his previous decision. He concludes, "Because this widow troubleth me . . . by her continual coming . . . I will avenge her" (18:5). He doesn't care at all for the widow's welfare or for justice, only for his own personal comfort. Pure selfishness motivates his decision: "Lest . . . she weary me" (18:5).

Jesus tells us to consider carefully what this unjust judge said—and did: "Hear what the unjust judge saith" (18:6). First, he finally gave the widow justice. Second, he did so because of her persistent petitioning, her continual coming. Thus the Lord teaches that we should imitate this woman and steadily petition God in patient faith until we receive our necessary answers.

But He draws a sharp contrast between God and the unjust judge: "Hear what the unjust judge saith. And shall not God avenge his own elect?" (18:7-8). God is like the judge in the parable in only two points:

> He is the higher authority whose intervention we seek.

> He responds to persistent intercession.

In no other point is God like him. The unjust judge is unfair and callous. God is just and compassionate. God's judgments are perfectly fair and His heart yearns to relieve His suffering children. So Jesus says, in effect, "If even an unjust judge will avenge his supplicants due to their persistence, shall not God, who is just and merciful, God, who has promised to deliver, God, who has always rescued His people of old, ultimately avenge you, even though He may sorely test your faith and patience before doing so?" Or as Abraham put it, "Shall not the Judge of all the earth do right?" (Genesis 18:25).

The most important statement in this parable from a prophetic viewpoint is the final statement. Jesus says, "Nevertheless, when the Son of man cometh, shall he find faith on the earth?" (18:8). By faith He does not mean our general belief in God—that God exists, the Bible is true, Jesus is the Son of God, God created the heavens and earth, etc. Rather, He means the faith under consideration in the context—confidence in the unerring justice of God. The thought is, "But when I come again, will this belief that God 'avenges His own elect' still be present?" Will Christians still believe that God is their Avenger? Will they still believe He overthrows oppressors and delivers the oppressed? Will they look to Him confidently for vindication in their personal conflicts? Will they continue to pray and wait for His righteous intervention even after long periods in which He seems indifferent toward them?

This is the question Jesus raises: *Will this belief still exist in the days just prior to His appearing?* Or "when the Son of man cometh," will the Laodicean generation be so saturated with lukewarm doctrine that Christians no longer believe their God capable of judgment?

Our generation has been flooded with talk of God's love. The soft side of the divine character has been greatly overemphasized while His other attributes have been almost totally ignored. All one hears about these days is God's grace, kindness, and tenderness. "But," you say, "is He not wondrously compassionate? Is He not love itself?" Of course, He is. But Christianity's concept of God's love has become iniquitous. Iniquitous doctrine is unequal truth—truth that has been twisted to give a false impression. It's incomplete information, an unbalanced description of God. We now believe that because God is love He automatically overlooks all sins and never sends punishments of any kind. God is love, but He is also holiness and perfect justice. And holiness is His chief attribute.

Two mighty prophets, Isaiah and the apostle John, beheld God in all His glory. The lasting impression made and duly recorded in their writings was not that of God's love but of His holiness. They each testified that angelic beings stand by His throne and ceaselessly praise Him for His holiness: "*Holy, holy, holy* is the Lord of hosts" (Isaiah 6:3; Revelation 4:8). This is not stated to undermine faith in God's mercy, but to establish the fact that He is first of all holy and, therefore, uncompromisingly just in His judgments.

Oswald Chambers taught, "God and love are synonymous . . . Whatever God is, love is. If your

215

conception of love does not agree with justice and judgment, purity and holiness, then your idea of love is wrong."

Forty years ago you rarely found a Christian who didn't believe in judgment—now you rarely find one who does. We believe He forgives, blesses, and prospers, yet draw back when it's asserted that He also chastens, opposes, and destroys. We're confident that He forgives the penitent, but unsure that He will punish the defiant. Yet His wrath is as dependable as His love and His justice as real as His forgiveness: "The Lord . . . will not at all acquit the wicked" (Nahum 1:3).

Many are discouraged because of the gross injustice of our times: "And because iniquity shall abound, the love of many shall grow cold" (Matthew 24:12). Murders go unpunished and their victims' rights ignored. Good men are ruined while the ungodly go on prospering. Hypocrites are praised while righteous men suffer reproach. Where is the God of justice in all this? He is bearing long with the righteous and hearing every cry for justice. While He tarries, their fruits of faith and long-suffering are being developed.

Others are afraid to confess their faith in a God of judgment lest they be accused of disbelief in the God of love. But the Master of love Himself, the compassionate Savior who hung from the Cross, declared emphatically that His Father and ours is utterly just and will one day avenge all His suffering servants: "And shall not God avenge his own elect? . . . I tell you that he will avenge them speedily" (Luke 18:7-8).

The wronged widow is a type of the righteous remnant of the last days. As she suffered injustice for a season, so God will permit all true disciples to experience a measure of mistreatment. She prayed persistently and so must we. She was avenged by the unjust judge and we will be avenged by Jesus when He appears: "For when they shall say, peace and safety, then sudden destruction cometh upon them . . . and they shall not escape" (1 Thessalonians 5:3).

The application of this prophetic parable is not limited to the great tribulation. It applies now to mistreated Christians as we await the Lord's appearing. It also applies to the Jewish and Gentile believers who will be persecuted during the first half of the tribulation. And it will apply finally to the hidden Jewish remnant in the latter half of the tribulation—those who suffer the antichrist's oppression as they await Christ's return to the earth (Revelation 12:14; 13:9-10).

God's temporary permission of injustice is not His approval of it. Beautiful divine justice will ultimately prevail. It must—our Lord has spoken. So don't faint. Keep believing firmly in the God of judgment. Come continually to your just and merciful Judge until He rises to deliver you from the forces and people that seek to destroy you. If you give God submission and trust now, He will one day give you justice and vindication: "For them who honor me I will honor" (1 Samuel 2:30).

> Many are the afflictions of the righteous; but
> the Lord delivereth him out of them all.
>
> (Psalms 34:19)

217